PMP® Examination Practice Questions for the *The PMBOK® Guide,* 5th edition.

Sean Whitaker, BA, MSc, MBA, PMP

ISBN-13: 978-1490578064
ISBN-10: 1490578064

CONTENTS

Introduction

Welcome, and congratulations!

You have either committed to taking the globe's leading project management credential or are considering it. Gaining the Project Management Professional (PMP®) certification is a great way to prove your existing experience, gain insight into best practice and advance your career prospects.

This book contains over 400 practice questions for the PMP® examination, based on the contents of the PMBOK® Guide, 5th edition. They are meant to provide revision and preparation for when you decide to sit the exam, as part of your overall study. It's a difficult exam and you'll need to make a significant investment in study time to make sure you pass.

You can use this book in any way you want. You can work through each of the questions in sequence, randomly pick ones from different chapters, or set yourself time limits to answer a particular set of questions.

Here are my 6 steps to help you answer the questions:

1. Read the question fully!

2. Reread the question!

3. Eliminate any obviously wrong answers.

4. Place the answers on a spectrum of most right to most wrong and choose the most right one.

5. Organize the answers in order of which would be done first to the one which would be done last, choose the one you would do first.

6. Guess! Leave no question unanswered.

No set of practice question can fully replicate the real exam. Examination preparation questions, like these, are focused on a single knowledge area, while many of the exam questions draw scenarios from several different process groups and knowledge areas. Be prepared for this and study the inputs into each process and where they originate as outputs. Additionally, study the outputs from each process and where they go as inputs. You will find outputs from processes in one knowledge area become inputs in an entirely separate knowledge area.

Here are some other study tips to increase your chances of passing the exam:

1. Start by finding out how you best learn. Some people can only learn by taking notes, or by reading and re-reading. You may learn better by drawing diagrams or by teaching to others. Visit a website like **www.vark-learn.com** to figure out how you learn best.

2. Use mnemonics to help you remember things. Mnemonics are phrases or acronyms that can jog your memory, like "**In Summer The Cruel Queen Has Cold Runny Porridge Snacks.**" The first letter of each word stands for the ten knowledge areas in the PMBOK® Guide: **In**tegration, **S**cope, **T**ime, **C**ost, **Q**uality, **H**uman Resource, **C**ommunications, **R**isk, **P**rocurement and **S**takeholder Management. You can use this one if it helps, or make up your own.

3. Plan your study well in advance and set aside time just for study. Stick to it. Life and work can get in the way of your best laid plans, but if you miss a scheduled study time be sure to make it up.

4. Teach the topic to someone, anyone! Teach it to your wife, husband, children, work colleagues, family pet or stuffed toy. Simply verbalizing and trying to explain in your own words to someone (or something else) will expose holes in your knowledge pretty fast.

5. Make games and puzzles of information that you have to learn. Write out processes on bits of card and throw them on the floor and try to reassemble them in the correct order.

6. Draw mind maps that link important concepts in a logical fashion.

7. Put together a study group of others aiming to sit the exam as well. Share ideas, experience and knowledge.

8. Use a commercial provider like Falcon Training (**www.falcontraining.com**) that has courses specifically designed to help you pass the exam. If Falcon Training isn't operating in your town, look for another PMI Registered Education Provider® (R.E.P.) to ensure you are getting a quality trainer.

9. Perhaps most importantly - get a book to help you with your self-study - I recommend the **PMP Training Kit** and **PMP Rapid Review** books by Sean Whitaker, both available from all good book retailers. Remember that although the PMBOK® Guide is still the best way to study for the exam, the exam itself is not based on the PMBOK® Guide but on the *PMP Examination Specification Outline* and so a book that covers all the material is much better than relying on the PMBOK® Guide.

Finally, it is important that if you get a question wrong, you understand why. Use the following sheet to record the reason you got a question wrong. See if you can spot patterns or issues that need adjusting in your test-taking technique.

With the benefit of hindsight I could have got more questions correct if I had…	
Carefully read the entire question and made sure I understood what was being asked.	
Carefully read all of the alternative answers provided and understood what each meant.	
Considered, and understood, all the answers before answering the question.	
Eliminated the obviously wrong answers.	
Had a thorough knowledge of the appropriate definitions from the PMBOK® Guide 4th edition.	
Had a working knowledge and understanding of the appropriate the relevant formula from the PMBOK® Guide 4th edition.	
Double checked my mathematical working out before selecting an answer.	
Answered the questions as per the PMBOK® Guide perspective instead of my own perspective.	
Reviewed my answer of tough questions after completing other related questions to see if my memory was any better.	
Had more time to complete the examination questions and didn't rush to answer each question.	

For all the up to date PMP® examination eligibility, pricing and scheduling information please visit the Project Management Institute website **www.pmi.org**.

Good luck!

Sean Whitaker

sean@seanwhitaker.com

P.S. please don't hesitate to contact me with any questions you may have, I'm always happy to hear from you and talk about project management.

Project Integration Management

1: Your team is confused because they use terminology and words in project communications that appear to be interchangeable, but other teams treat them as though they have specific, unique meanings. How can your team find out what the terms mean?

A. The best way to differentiate between similar project terms is to ask the project sponsor

B. Direct your team to a defined and standardized glossary such as the PMBOK® Guide

C. Have your project team vote on what definitions they would like to use for common terms

D. Project management terms have different meanings in different countries, so consult your nearest PMI community.

2: A project can be considered to be ended under all of the following conditions EXCEPT

A. When the project manager resigns

B. When the project objectives have been achieved

C. When the project is terminated because its objectives will not or cannot be met

D. When the need for the project no longer exists

3: What is the BEST definition of a project?

A. The ongoing management of a business enterprise to achieve profitability

B. A body of work constrained by finances and time

C. An organized effort of work by a team managed by a project manager

D. A temporary endeavor undertaken to create a unique product, service or result

4: Which of the following is NOT an example of a project?

A. Building a new house
B. Regularly achieving 3% growth on last year's sales figures
C. Designing a new software solution
D. Implementing a new business process or procedure

5: Which of the following is NOT one of the 5 process groups in the PMBOK® Guide ?

A. Executing
B. Closing
C. Initiating
D. Checking

6: You are the project manager on a project to develop a new piece of customer management software for an external client. Through your approved change control process you are considering a request to alter the scope of the project. While considering the impact of the request upon the project scope you must also consider the impact upon other areas of the project such as quality, schedule, budget and risk. These other areas that you are considering represent what to the project?

A. Risks
B. Opportunities
C. Constrictions
D. Constraints

7: The process of continuously improving and detailing a project management plan, or parts of a project management plan, as more specific information becomes available is known as what?

A. Project life cycle
B. Progressive elaboration
C. Continuous improvement
D. Iterative expectation management

8: Portfolio management is BEST defined as what?

A. A group of related projects managed in a coordinated way
B. A group of projects managed by a project director
C. A collection of projects grouped together to take advantage of effective management to meet strategic business objectives
D. A collection of projects relating to a single business unit within an organization

9: A group of related projects is known as what?

A. Portfolio
B. Program
C. PMO
D. Life Cycle

10: Which of the following is NOT a strategic consideration for authorizing a project?

A. Customer demand
B. Strategic opportunity
C. Return on investment
D. Market demand

11: A body assigned responsibility for the centralized and coordinated management of projects within an organization is known as what?

A. War room
B. Program management office
C. Project headquarters
D. Project management office

12: Which of the following is NOT a primary function of a project management office?

A. Managing shared resources across several projects
B. Providing a project manager with daily progress reports
C. Identifying and developing project management methodology, best practices and standards
D. Coordinating communication across projects

13: All of the following are points where projects can intersect with operational activity at various points during the product life cycle EXCEPT

A. During development of a new product
B. While monitoring and controlling
C. During improvements in operations
D. At closeout phases

14: What is the best description of the relationship between project management and organizational strategy?

A. Organizational strategy will ensure the projects are delivered successfully due to the way in which it appoints a qualified project manager
B. Organizational strategy enable a project manager to provide appropriate governance to the entire project life cycle.
C. Organizational strategy and project management don't interact as one is operational in nature and the other is project based
D. Organizational strategy should provide guidance and direction to project management and project management should deliver organizational strategy by successful project delivery

15: What is the BEST definition of business value?

A. The value of all the projects that the company is currently completing

B. The value added to the business by projects that are completed successfully

C. The value of the tangible assets the company holds that can be liquidated to provide working capital

D. The value of the total sum of all tangible and intangible elements of the business

16: What is the BEST definition of the role of the project manager?

A. The person responsible for sharing resources among projects

B. The person responsible for delivery of technical tasks

C. The person responsible for budget control

D. The person assigned by the performing organization to achieve the project objectives

17: All of the following are examples of enterprise environmental factors EXCEPT

A. Government or industry standards or regulations

B. Political climate

C. Net present value of investment

D. Project management information systems

18: What does OPM3 measure?

A. The interdependency of projects within a program of work

B. The level of variance between project management best practice and the actual application

C. The ability of a project manager to successfully deliver a project

D. An organization's project management maturity level

19: The internal and external environmental factors that both surround and influence a project are known as what?

A. Environmental process assets
B. Enterprise environmental factors
C. Environmental enterprise constraints
D. Enterprise organizational assets

20: The collection of generally sequential and sometimes overlapping project phases is known as what?

A. Project management methodology
B. Project life cycle
C. Project management office
D. Project management information systems

21: All of the following are characteristics of the project life cycle EXCEPT?

A. Checking the project work
B. Closing the project
C. Starting the project
D. Carrying out the project work

22: Cost and staffing levels are typically highest at what point in the project life cycle?

A. Organizing and preparing
B. Carrying out the work
C. Starting the project
D. Closing the project

23: The ability of stakeholders to influence the project is greatest at which point in the project?

A. During the project execution
B. At the close of the project
C. At the beginning of the project
D. It is equal throughout a project

24: The cost of changes to a project is greatest at what point in a project's time line?

A. It is equal throughout a project
B. At the beginning of the project
C. During the project execution
D. Towards the end of the project

25: Divisions within a project where extra control is needed to effectively manage the completion of a major deliverable are known as what?

A. Sub-projects
B. Stage gates
C. Decision trees
D. Phases

26: Which of the following is NOT an example of a phase-to-phase relationship?

A. Overlapping
B. Progressive
C. Iterative
D. Sequential

27: A person or organization whose interest may be affected by the project is called what?

A. Team member
B. Customer
C. Stakeholder
D. Sponsor

28: You are the project manager working in an organization where the functional manager, that some of your staff answer to when not working on your project, controls the project budget and resource availability. This type of organization is commonly referred to as what?

A. Weak matrix
B. Strong matrix
C. Functional
D. Projectized

29: You work in an organization where staff members are grouped according to their specialty such as production, engineering and accounting and projects are generally undertaken within these respective groupings. What is this type of organizational structure known as?

A. Functional
B. Weak matrix
C. Strong matrix
D. Projectized

30: All of the following are examples of Organizational Process Assets EXCEPT

A. A template for a work breakdown structure
B. Lessons learned from previous projects
C. Government regulations
D. Configuration management knowledge bases

31: The process of determining which the PMBOK® Guide processes are appropriate and the appropriate degree of rigor to be applied in any given project is known as what?

A. Standardization
B. Prudency
C. Customizing
D. Tailoring

32: The process group consisting of those processes performed to define a new project or a new phase of an existing project by obtaining authorization to start the project or phase is known as what?

A. Executing
B. Initiating
C. Closing
D. Planning

33: You are completing the work defined in the project management plan to satisfy the project specifications. Which process group would your activities fall under?

A. Monitoring and controlling
B. Planning
C. Initiating
D. Executing

34: How many processes are there in the Project Integration Management knowledge area in the PMBOK® Guide?

A. 6
B. 5
C. 4
D. 7

35: You are in involved in making choices about resource allocation on your project, making trade-offs among competing objectives and alternatives and managing the interdependencies among the different project management knowledge areas. Of which the PMBOK® Guide knowledge area will it be most useful to have an in-depth understanding?

A. Develop Project Management Plan
B. Project Integration Management
C. Project Risk Management
D. Perform Integrated Change Control

**36: The knowledge and processes described in the PMBOK®
Guide should be applied in what way?**

A. You should apply all the different knowledge areas and
processes to your project at the level required to achieve project
success
B. Rigorously and exactly as shown in the PMBOK® Guide
C. The PMBOK® Guide is only a guide and you should only apply
the parts you understand fully
D. You should apply the project management knowledge, skills and
required processes in whatever order is appropriate and with
varying degrees of rigor to achieve the desired project performance

**37: You are newly appointed to a project and are currently reading
the project charter to gain an understanding of what is known
about the project at this point. The project charter should contain
enough information to do all of the following EXCEPT**

A. Appoint the project manager
B. Initiate the project
C. Describe the high level project scope
D. Complete the WBS

**38: You have been called in to evaluate a project that is
experiencing some performance challenges. The team seems
disorganized, and when you ask to meet the project sponsor, the
project manager replies that she doesn't know who the sponsor is.
She also shares with you that the planned value (PV) is $20,000,
earned value (EV) is $14,500 and actual cost (AC) is $36,000. You
decide that you should really go back to the beginning and figure
how this project got started. What document should you request?**

A. The project authorization memo
B. The project plan
C. The cost performance analysis and report
D. The project charter

39: You and your team are currently developing the project charter and are looking for valuable inputs you can use to complete it. All of the following are inputs in the Develop Project Charter process EXCEPT

A. Enterprise environmental factors
B. Business case
C. Project management plan
D. Project statement of work

40: Which of the following would you expect to see in the business case contained within a project charter?

A. A copy of the stakeholder register
B. A description of the expected market demand for the product of the project
C. Any blank templates your organization has to assist in completing the project charter
D. The project management plan

41: What is the high level narrative description of products or services to be delivered by the project more commonly referred to as?

A. Product scope description
B. Project scope statement
C. Project scope
D. Project statement of work

42: Which of the following is not a method you would expect to see used in a business case to justify a project on financial grounds?

A. Net present value (NPV)
B. Return on investment (ROI)
C. External rate of investment (ERI)
D. Internal rate of return (IRR)

43: You are a project manager working for an organization and have been asked to help evaluate some potential projects and draft the statement of work (SOW) to be given to potential solution providers. One of the projects has an expected value of $50,000 in 3 years. Another project has an expected value of $60,000 in 4 years. The discount rate is 8.2%. You will want to make sure your statement of work indicates all the following EXCEPT

A. High level project scope description
B. Business need
C. Staffing plan
D. Strategic plan

44: Which of the following is a tools or technique used during the Develop Project Charter process?

A. Business case preparation
B. Delphi technique
C. Analytical techniques
D. Expert judgment

45: You have just taken over a project that has been underway for 10 months. The previous project manager left the project for health reasons. The project is performing well but you would like to become familiar with the way in which this particular project is being executed, monitored and controlled, and closed. What document will help you in this instance?

A. Quality management plan
B. Project statement of work
C. Project charter
D. Project management plan

46: You and your team are carrying out the development of the project management plan for your project. You are unsure about which inputs are best to use to develop it. All of the following are inputs into the Develop Project Management Plan process EXCEPT

A. Communications management plan
B. Project charter
C. Process improvement plan
D. Work performance information

47: After completing most of your project management plan, your project sponsor is so impressed that she comments, "With this level of planning and detail, we know exactly where the project will be nine months from now." What is the BEST response you should give to the sponsor?

A. These are exactly the type of results that are achieved through professional project management as defined in the PMBOK® Guide.
B. Projects that are planned and scheduled using the Critical Chain Method will completely eliminate any possible changes.
C. That's correct. Good planning gives us precise knowledge about how our project will perform.
D. Projects seldom run exactly according to the project management plan, which is why we have the integrated change control process.

48: All of the following are characteristics of a project management plan EXCEPT

A. The project management plan describes how work will be executed to accomplish the project objectives
B. The project management plan can be either summary or detailed
C. The project management plan sets out the business case for the project, the project manager and approval from the project sponsor
D. The project management plan integrates and consolidates all of the subsidiary management plans

49: How would you BEST characterize the project management plan?

A. The project management plan includes the actions necessary to define, integrate, and coordinate all subsidiary plans into a project management plan. The content will vary depending upon the complexity of the project.
B. The project management plan includes the actions necessary to define, integrate, and coordinate all subsidiary plans into a project management plan. The content will be very similar regardless of the complexity of the project.
C. The project management plan includes the actions necessary to define, integrate, and coordinate all subsidiary plans into a project management plan. This is a deliverable that is rarely used in real practice.
D. The project management plan includes the actions necessary to define, integrate, and coordinate all subsidiary plans into a project management plan. The content will be very high level and further refined in the project charter.

50: Which of the following is a tool or technique used during the Develop Project Management Plan process?

A. Project scope analysis
B. Project management information systems
C. Expert judgment
D. Business case preparation

51: The performance measurement baseline is most commonly a combination of what other baselines?

A. Communications, cost, and schedule baselines
B. Schedule, cost, and risk baselines
C. Scope, schedule, and cost baselines
D. Procurement, scope, and cost baselines

52: Implementing approved changes to a project includes all of the following EXCEPT

A. Lessons learned
B. Preventative action
C. Corrective action
D. Defect repair

53: The activities involved in performing the work defined in the project management plan to achieve the project's objectives include all of the following EXCEPT

A. Complete the business case and use it as an input into the development of the project charter
B. Manage risks and implement risk response activities
C. Staff, train, and manage the team members assigned to the project
D. Issue change requests and adapt approved changes into the project's scope, plan, and environment

54: Which of the following is NOT an input into the Direct and Manage Project Work process?

A. Project management plan
B. Work performance data
C. Approved change requests
D. Enterprise environmental factors

55: Which of the following is NOT an example of an organizational process asset used in the Direct and Manage Project Work process?

A. Issue and defect management procedures
B. Process measurement database
C. Stakeholder risk tolerances
D. Standardized guidelines and work instructions

56: You are the sponsor on a time constrained project that must deliver the expected output by a defined date or your organization will face severe financial penalties. You meet with the project manager 20 days after the kick-off of the project and ask to have an update on schedule progress, schedule activities that have been started and the extent to which quality standards are being met. The project manager looks at you somewhat uncomfortably and tells you that he doesn't have any of that information. What output from Direct and Manage Project Work is the project manager missing?

A. Work performance data
B. Project management plan updates
C. Deliverables
D. Change requests

57: The process of tracking, reviewing, and regulating the progress of your project to meet the performance objectives defined in the project management plan is known as what?

A. Monitor and Control Project Work
B. Direct and Manage Project Work
C. Perform Integrated Change Control
D. Develop Project Management Plan

58: Which of the following is NOT a tool or technique used during the Monitor and Control Project Work process?

A. Meetings
B. Expert judgment
C. Analytical techniques
D. Delphi technique

59: Which of the following is NOT an output of the Monitor and Control Project Work process?

A. Project documents updates
B. Project management plan updates
C. Change requests
D. Work performance information

60: You and your team are considering making an early change to a part of the project management plan, when one of your team members says that it is too early to be considering any changes. At what points in the project would you perform integrated change control?

A. During project execution
B. From project inception to completion
C. During project monitoring and control
D. From project execution through to project closure

61: All of the following are characteristics of a change request EXCEPT

A. Every documented change request must be approved or rejected
B. All change requests should be considered by the change control board
C. They may be initiated verbally
D. They may involve assessing impacts on several knowledge areas

62: You have developed a formal documented procedure to assist with technical and administrative direction, control and iteration management of project documents, records, physical characteristics and required materials. What is this procedure called?

A. A risk management system
B. A configuration management system
C. A PMIS
D. A work authorization system

63: Project-wide application of the configuration management system accomplished three main objectives. Which of the following is NOT one of these objectives?

A. Provides opportunities to continuously validate and improve the project by considering the impact of each change
B. Establishes an evolutionary method to consistently identify and request changes to established baselines
C. Provides a documented process to enable the assessment of requested changes to the project
D. Provides a mechanism for the project management team to consistently communicate all approved and rejected changes to the stakeholders

64: The configuration management system is a collection of formal documented procedures. Which of the following is NOT an objective of configuration management?

A. Record and report each change to the functional characteristics
B. Prevent any changes to functional characteristics
C. Identify and document the functional characteristics of a product
D. Support the audit of the products to verify conformance to requirements

65: All of the following are configuration management activities included in the Perform Integrated Change Control process EXCEPT

A. Configuration identification
B. Configuration control and assessment
C. Configuration status accounting
D. Configuration verification and audit

66: As an experienced project manager, you have been asked to review a project with an SPI of 0.86 and a CPI of 0.83. You quickly identify a number of changes that are required to fix defects and meet some critical customer needs. Which Project Integration Management Process will you need to perform?

A. Develop Project Management Plan
B. Direct and Manage Project Work
C. Monitor and Control Project Work
D. Perform Integrated Change Control

67: Which of the following is NOT an input into the Perform Integrated Change Control process?

A. Work performance reports
B. Change requests
C. Organizational process assets
D. Project documents updates

68: If a change request is considered feasible but outside the project scope, what should occur if the change is approved?

A. The person making the change request should be removed from the project to avoid conflict of interest
B. The request should not be approved
C. The project sponsor should be consulted
D. The relevant baseline will require changing

69: All of the following are characteristics of the Close Project or Phase process EXCEPT

A. It is the process of closing and finalizing any contracts for providing goods or services
B. It is the process of finalizing all activities across all of the project management process groups
C. It establishes the procedures to investigate and documents the reasons for actions taken if a project is terminated before completion
D. It includes all of the activities necessary for administrative closure of the project or phase

70: Which of the following is NOT an input into the Close Project or Phase process?

A. Organizational process assets
B. Accepted deliverables
C. Work performance information
D. Project management plan

71: You are a project manager and have just been informed that due to budget cuts your project has been cancelled and your team should cease work immediately. The project was doing very well and will likely be restarted at a later time when organizational finances are better. What is the BEST action to take next?

A. Release your team to the functional organization, shred most of your documents, and ask for a new project
B. Ignore the request since your charter has been approved and commits organizational resources to you project
C. Formally document why the project was terminated and set up the procedures to transfer finished and unfinished deliverables to others
D. See if more money is available from another project

72: You are just about to complete administrative closure of your project and are updating the relevant organizational process assets for your company. Which of the following is NOT an example of an organizational process asset that you would update?

A. Historical information
B. Project files
C. Project closure documents
D. Stakeholder risk tolerance register

73: Your project is reporting a CPI of 1.02 and a SPI of 1.1. The project you are delivering is for a customer who is notoriously difficult to please. Your team comes up with a way to deliver more functionality in the project than the customer is expecting at a lower cost and the change will result in improvements to the schedule. What is your BEST course of action?

A. Carry out the work and surprise the customer
B. Do not do the extra work as it is not included in the project scope
C. Contact the customer and explain the situation to them
D. Do not do the extra work as the customer will not appreciate it

74: You are a project manager that is involved with the preparation of a business case to justify whether a particular project should go ahead. You are using net present value as a key financial filter. Your project will spend $100,000 in the first year then generate revenue of $33,000 in the second year, $62,000 in the third year, and $85,000 in the third year. Assuming an interest rate of 10% what is the net present value?

A. $41 000
B. $100 000
C. $80 000
D. $280 000

100K spend
180K revenues
— got to be less than 80K!

75: You are choosing between two potential projects that your organisation could undertake. The first project, Project Eagle, will cost $500,000 and will have an NPV of $50,000. The second project, Project Falcon, will cost $420,000 and will have an NPV of $48,000. Which of the two projects should you do?

A. Project Eagle
B. Project Falcon
C. Do not have enough information to answer this question.
D. Neither project meets NPV criteria

76: After measuring expected project benefits, your project management office has four projects from which to choose. Project A has a Net Present Value of $160,000 and will cost $10,000. Project B has a Net Present Value of $470,000 and will cost $220,000. Project C has a Net Present Value of $265,000 and will cost $33,000. Project D has a Net Present Value of $335,000, and will cost $57,000. Which project would be BEST?

A. Project B
B. Project A
C. Project C
D. Project D

77: You are assisting your portfolio manger in making a decision about which of two possible projects should be given approval to proceed. Project A would generate $75,000 in benefit. Project B would generate $225,000 in benefit. Unfortunately due to limited resources, your company can only perform one of these and they choose Project B because of the higher benefit. What is the opportunity cost of performing Project B?

A. $300,000
B. $225,000
C. $75,000
D. $150,000

78: The processes required to ensure that the project includes all the work and only the work required to complete the project successfully are known as what?

A. Project scope management
B. Project baseline delivery
C. Project specification delivery
D. Project management execution

Project Scope Management

79: You are completing the work defined in the project scope statement of a new software development project when a team member points out that you have an opportunity to deliver enhanced capability to the client at no extra cost, time or risk to the project. What should you do NEXT?

A. Ask the team member to keep quiet about the changes and ignore their request as it presents too many risks to the project
B. Decline to make the changes and proceed to deliver exactly what the scope statement sets out
C. Go ahead and make the changes and surprise the client with the extra capability
D. Assess the change via the change control process and if approved amend the project scope statement

80: You are new to a project that has been underway for some time. One of your first jobs as project manager is to familiarize yourself with, and understand the scope baseline. What documents make up the scope baseline?

A. The WBS, the project management plan, and the change register
B. The project scope statement, the WBS, and the risk register
C. The WBS, the change register, and the project scope statement
D. The project scope statement, the WBS and the WBS dictionary

81: You are a project manager and you are working with your sponsor to define and plan a complex project. You plan to complete your initiation and planning documents sequentially to make sure the organization really understands and supports the project. What key deliverables will you produce in the correct order?

A. Project management plan, project charter, project scope statement
B. Project charter, requirements documentation, project scope statement
C. Project charter, project scope statement, requirements documentation
D. Project management plan, requirements documentation, project charter

82: What is the name of the planning document that describes how requirements will be analyzed, documented and managed?

A. Requirements traceability matrix
B. Scope management plan
C. Requirements management plan
D. Requirements scope statement

83: Completion of the project scope is measured against the scope management plan. Completion of the product scope is measured against what?

A. Product requirements
B. Scope management plan
C. Project management plan
D. Client expectations

84: The difference between project requirements and product requirements is what?

A. Project requirements can include tools and techniques for completing the appropriate project process groups, while product requirements can include the method of delivery and manufacturing quality specifications

B. Project requirements can include business requirements, project management requirements and delivery requirements, while product requirements can include technical requirements, security requirements and performance requirements

C. Project requirements relate to the detail included in the project management plan while product requirements are defined by the client's expectations

D. Project requirements relate to the detail contained in the individual components of the project management plan and the processes that make them up, while product requirements relate to the specifications provided by the client and their expectations for

85: The process of defining and documenting stakeholders' needs to meet the project objectives is known as what?

A. Collect requirements
B. Project integration management
C. Project scope management
D. Determine stakeholder expectations

86: A team member on your project has questioned whether or not the project is delivering as per the original high level requirements and narrative high level product description, and is concerned that what you are doing has deviated from this. What is your BEST course of action?

A. Have the team member assigned to another project as he or she is clearly not a team player
B. Check the project management plan
C. Check the project scope statement
D. Check the project charter

87: All of the following are tools or techniques for completing the Collect Requirements process EXCEPT

A. Focus groups
B. Requirements traceability matrix
C. Group decision making techniques
D. Interviews

88: You have decided to use a technique to help get a comprehensive set of project requirements that involves getting a group of experts to answer a series of questionnaires anonymously and provide feedback on information received in an iterative manner. What technique are you using?

A. The Delphi technique
B. Nominal group technique
C. Brainstorming
D. Mind mapping

89: The requirements documentation is an output of which process?

A. Scope Definition
B. Develop Project Charter
C. Project Scope Management
D. Collect Requirements

90: All of the following are components of the requirements documentation EXCEPT

A. Business rules stating the guiding principles of the organization
B. Business need
C. Acceptance criteria
D. Configuration management activities

91: You are a project manager working on a complex construction project and have begun the process of planning your project. You have the project charter which is guiding you in preparing your project management plan. Using your requirements documentation you begin the process of developing a detailed description of the project and product. What process are you completing?

A. Collect Requirements
B. Define Scope
C. Plan Scope Management
D. Define Activities

92: You are the project manager for a large project and have recently taken over the project from another project manager. Upon review of the project schedule, you learn that two major deliverables are missing. Your sponsor reminds you how important it is to complete this project on time and within budget. What part of Scope Management was likely not done properly and should be reviewed and perhaps even repeated?

A. Stakeholder analysis
B. Critical path analysis
C. Integrated change control
D. Decomposition

93: Which of the following is NOT an input into the Define Scope process?

A. Organizational process assets
B. Project charter
C. Requirements documentation
D. Project scope statement

94: You have been assigned as a new project manager for a multi-phase project that is midway through phase 3 of 5 phases. While the overall work of the team seems pretty good, you feel that phase 3 is starting to drift from the original plan. You set up a meeting with the project sponsor to discuss your concerns. The sponsor is surprised and agrees that phase 3 includes work that was not documented in the original agreement. To prove this, the sponsor reaches refers you to which document?

A. Project scope statement
B. Project management plan
C. Statement of work
D. Requirements traceability matrix

95: You and your project team have spent time decomposing the project scope statement using a work breakdown structure template your organization has. What is the lowest level of the Work Breakdown Structure called?

A. Tasks
B. Work packages
C. Activities
D. Units

96: The PMBOK® Guide process of subdividing project deliverables and project work into smaller components is known as what?

A. Create WBS
B. Define Activities
C. Define Scope
D. Collect Requirements

97: All of the following are true about the work breakdown structure EXCEPT

A. The planned work within the lowest levels can be scheduled, cost estimated, monitored, and controlled
B. It is a deliverable-oriented hierarchical decomposition of the work to be executed by the project team, to accomplish the project objectives and create the required deliverables
C. Each descending level of the WBS represents an increasingly detailed definition of the project work
D. It is an output of the Define Scope process

98: The point in the decomposition of the WBS at which cost and activity durations for the work can be reliably estimated and managed is called what?

A. Work packages
B. Activities
C. WBS dictionary elements
D. Tasks

99: Excessive decomposition of the WBS can lead to all of the following EXCEPT

A. Non-productive management effort
B. Inefficient use of resources
C. Decreased efficiency in performing the work
D. Added value

100: You have a new team member on board and she is new to the profession of project management. How would you explain the work breakdown structure to her

A. The WBS is a hierarchically organized depiction of the resources by type to be used on the project
B. The WBS represents the work specified in the current approved project scope statement
C. The WBS defines the scope of the contract
D. The WBS is a list of categories and sub-categories within which risks may arise for a typical project

101: Your project team has largely completed the creation of the WBS. However some deliverables have not been decomposed because clarity is lacking. The project team decides to leave these and wait until more details are available. What is this an example of?

A. Poor project management planning
B. Progressive decision making
C. Iterative expectation management
D. Rolling wave planning

102: You are having trouble understanding some of the detail associated with your WBS work packages. To help you understand the components of your WBS in greater detail, which document would you use?

A. Project charter
B. WBS dictionary
C. Project scope statement
D. Activity list

103: How does scope validation differ from quality control?

A. Scope validation is primarily concerned with ensuring the scope management plan is being followed while quality control is ensuring that the product is fit for purpose
B. Scope validation involves checking the output from the project, whereas quality control means checking the output from the product
C. Scope validation is primarily concerned with acceptance of the deliverables, while quality control is primarily concerned with correctness of the deliverables and meeting the quality requirements specific for the deliverables
D. Scope validation involves checking that the requirements documentation reflects the project charter whereas quality control means checking the amount of defects in the deliverable

104: Validate Scope is the process of doing what?

A. Accepting approved change requests and amending the project scope baseline
B. Finalizing the project and product scope statement
C. Performing variance analysis on the expected and actual deliverables
D. Formalizing acceptance of the completed project deliverables

105: You are using your project management plan, requirements documentation, requirements traceability matrix and undertaking inspection to validate the project and product. What process group are you involved in?

A. Monitoring and controlling
B. Closing
C. Planning
D. Executing

106: The customer has contacted you and has requested a change to the scope of your project, which is already well underway. They are in a hurry to get the change implemented and they tell you that they are prepared to pay whatever extra cost is associated with the change so you should just get on and do it. What is your BEST course of action?

A. Refer to your change control process for controlling scope and submit the request as detailed
B. Tell the customer it is too late as the scope is already defined
C. Incorporate the change into the project as the customer has agreed to it
D. Send the customer a written agreement for them to sign before you accept the change into the project

107: Your team is receiving a large number of small change requests and some are being adopted without being fully documented and assessed. These uncontrolled scope changes are often referred to as what?

A. Scope change
B. Scope variance
C. Scope creep
D. Scope amendment

108: What document shows how requirements activities will be planned, tracked and changed?

A. Change control plan
B. Requirements management plan
C. Project management plan
D. Scope management plan

109: You are assessing the magnitude of variation from the original scope baseline. What technique are you utilizing?

A. Scope baseline analysis
B. Change control assessment
C. Variance analysis
D. Variation change analysis

110: What is the difference between Validate Scope and Quality Control?

A. Quality Control is concerned with the correct acceptance of the deliverables; Validate Scope is concerned with the completeness of the deliverables
B. Quality Control is concerned with the correctness of the deliverables; Validate Scope is concerned with the acceptance of the deliverables
C. Quality Control is performed in the Monitoring & Controlling part of the project, while Validate Scope is performed at the Executing part of the project
D. Validate Scope is performed by the Project Sponsor, while Quality Control is performed by the team members

Project Time Management

111: What is the generally correct order of schedule development activities in the Time Management knowledge area?

A. Define Activities, Sequence Activities, Estimate Activity Resources, Estimate Activity Durations, Develop Schedule
B. Sequence Activities, Develop Schedule, Estimate Activity Resources, Estimate Activity Durations, Define Activities
C. Define Activities, Estimate Activity Resources, Estimate Activity Durations, Sequence Activities, Develop Schedule
D. Sequence Activities, Define Activities, Estimate Activity Resources, Estimate Activity Durations, Develop Schedule

112: You are using the work packages from your WBS to assist with creating your project schedule. You begin breaking the work packages down in to the actual work necessary to complete the work package. What are you in the process of defining?

A. Work package assignments
B. Project tasks
C. WBS dictionary items
D. Activities

113: You are the project manager on a project that is currently in the planning stage. You are working on your project schedule and beginning the process of defining your activity list. Involving your team members in this process would result in what outcome?

A. Better and more accurate results
B. Project inefficiencies due to delays experienced in building consensus
C. Bad team morale due to disagreements between experts
D. Extra cost to the project

114: You have your activity list completed and are explaining to your team members what it contains. Which of the following is NOT contained in the activity list?

A. Milestone list
B. Scope of work description
C. All schedule activities required on the project
D. Activity identifier

115: You and your project management team are conducting the activity sequencing for a new project. The team has determined that Task A takes 3 days. Task B is dependent upon Task A finishing and has a duration of 1 day. Task C takes 4 days. Task D is dependent upon Task C starting and has a duration of 7 days. Task E is dependent upon both Task C and Task D finishing and has a duration of 2 days. Task F is dependent upon both Task E and Task B finishing and has a duration of 4 days. What is the duration of the project?

A. 13 days
B. 10 days
C. 17 days
D. 8 days

116: Which of the following is the most commonly used type of precedence relationship?

A. Start-to-finish
B. Finish-to-start
C. Finish-to-finish
D. Start-to-start

117: You are using the precedence diagramming method to construct your project schedule network diagram. What other name is used to describe the precedence diagramming method?

A. Critical chain methodology
B. Activity on Arrow
C. Activity on node
D. Critical path methodology

118: After talking with your team and the people responsible for completing the activity you have scheduled two activities in your project so that the successor activity is able to start a week before the predecessor activity. This is an example of what?

A. Slack
B. Lag
C. Lead
D. Float

119: What is the difference between a lead and a lag?

A. A lead means a successor activity can be started prior to the completion of a predecessor activity. A lag directs a delay in the successor activity.
B. A lead means that both activities can start at the same time. A lag means that neither can start until the other one starts.
C. A lead means that the successor activity must start prior to the predecessor activity finishes. A lag means the successor activity has a mandatory dependency and can not start until the predecessor activity is complete.
D. A lead means the amount of time free on the critical path between activities. A lag is the amount of delay that can occur between activities that will not adversely affect the final project delivery date

120: You are completing the sequence of activities and note that one of your activities can not proceed until consent is granted by the local government agency. This is an example of what sort of dependency?

A. Discretionary
B. External
C. Environmental
D. Mandatory

121: The project schedule network diagram is the primary output of which process?

A. Sequence activities
B. Define activities
C. Develop schedule
D. Control schedule

122: A resource calendar includes what sort of information?

A. The dates of annual holidays for project team members
B. When and how long project resources will be available during the project
C. The duration of each activity in the project resource diagram
D. The length of time the project will require input from external resources

123: You are estimating your activity resources and breaking down the work within each activity to its lowest level then aggregating these estimates to get a total quantity for each activity's resources. What tool or technique are you using?

A. Bottom-up estimating
B. Published estimating data
C. Expert judgment
D. Parametric Estimating

124: All of the following are inputs into the Estimate Activity Duration process EXCEPT

A. Activity list
B. Activity attributes
C. Project scope statement
D. Activity duration estimates

125: While estimating the activity durations on your project you come across a similar project completed by your organization last year. To save time you use information from this project to help you estimate your activity durations. This is an example of which tool or technique?

A. Analogous Estimating
B. Bottom-Up estimating
C. Parametric Estimating
D. Three point estimating

126: As a result of a brainstorming session your team determines that the most likely duration of an activity will be 8 days, the optimistic duration is 6 days and the pessimistic duration is 16 days. What it the expected activity duration?

A. 30 days
B. 5 days
C. 10 days
D. 9 Days

127: There is some uncertainty over the duration for a particular activity on your project. You call your team together who all have experience in completing the activity and after a brainstorming session they are able to determine a most likely duration, an optimistic duration and a pessimistic duration. You then use these numbers to calculate the expected activity duration. This is an example of which sort of tool or technique?

A. Parametric Estimating
B. Bottom-Up estimating
C. Analogous Estimating
D. Three point estimating

128: To estimate the amount of time it will take to install 500 meters of cable on your project you divide the number of meters required by how many meters an hour the person laying the cable can lay. This is an example of which sort of tool or technique?

A. Parametric Estimating
B. Bottom-Up estimating
C. Analogous Estimating
D. Three point estimating

129: All of the following are inputs into the Develop Schedule process EXCEPT

A. Project schedule network diagrams
B. Project schedule
C. Activity list
D. Resource calendars

130: The process of analyzing activity sequences, durations, resource requirements and scheduled constraints to create the project schedule is called what?

A. Project schedule development
B. Create project schedule
C. Develop schedule
D. Schedule management

131: You are completing a network diagram with the following information: Task A has a duration of 3 days and has the start as a predecessor; Task B has a duration of 5 days and also has the start as a predecessor; Task C has a duration of 4 days and has task A as a predecessor; Task D has a duration of 4 days and has task B as a predecessor; Task E has a duration of 6 days and has tasks C & D as predecessors; Task F has a duration of 5 days and has task D as a predecessor; the finish milestone has a duration of zero days and has tasks E & F as predecessors. Using this data what is the duration of the project?

A. 13
B. 14
C. 15
D. 16

132: You are completing a network diagram with the following information: Task A has a duration of 3 days and has the start as a predecessor; Task B has a duration of 5 days and also has the start as a predecessor; Task C has a duration of 4 days and has task A as a predecessor; Task D has a duration of 4 days and has task B as a predecessor; Task E has a duration of 6 days and has tasks C & D as predecessors; Task F has a duration of 5 days and has task D as a predecessor; the finish milestone has a duration of zero days and has tasks E & f as predecessors. What is the critical path for this network diagram?

A. Start-A-C-E-Finish
B. Start-B-D-F-Finish
C. Start-B-D-E-Finish
D. Start-A-C-F-Finish

133: According to Goldratt's critical chain theory in order to reduce risk in schedules a project manager should

A. Start activities in the critical chains as early as possible
B. Start activities in the feeder chains as late as possible
C. Add buffer to the critical chains
D. Start activities in the feeder chains as early as possible

134: Which of these statements about the critical path method and the critical chain method is FALSE?

A. The critical chain method initially uses non-conservative estimates, whereas the critical path method is concerned with using more accurate estimates
B. The critical chain method accounts for resource availability, whereas the critical path method does not
C. The critical path method focuses on managing the total float of network paths, whereas the critical chain method focuses on managing the buffer activity durations and the resources applied to planned schedule activities
D. The critical path method schedules early start and late start dates to planned activities, whereas the critical chain method schedules only late start dates to planned activities

135: You are adding in duration buffers that are non-workable schedule activities to manage uncertainty into your project schedule. What tool or technique are you using?

A. Critical chain method
B. Critical path method
C. Three point estimating
D. Parametric estimating

136: You are using a methodology that calculates the amount of float on various paths in the network diagram to determine the minimum project duration. What tool or technique are you using?

A. Critical chain method
B. Critical path method
C. Parametric estimating
D. Three point estimating

137: In the first attempt at resource leveling the project schedule, what would you expect to occur?

A. The number of required resources will increase during certain time periods of the project
B. The number of required resources will decrease during certain time periods of the project
C. The overall project duration will increase
D. The overall project duration will decrease

138: You are the project manager on a software project and while examining your schedule you see that there has been a delay in completing a task. The sensible choice seems to move a person from another task who is an expert on the work that is behind. There is a choice of using two different people who are working on two different tasks. One person is working on a task that has five days of free float and the other is working on a task that has eight days of total float and no free float. What is your BEST course of action?

A. The person working on the task with free float of five days
B. The person working on the task with total float of eight days
C. Either person can be used
D. A person should be brought in from outside the project

139: You are using a technique that examines the possible outcomes if a particular situation occurs. What is this technique called?

A. Critical chain methodology
B. Schedule compression
C. What-if scenario analysis
D. Parametric Estimating

140: Your project team is behind schedule and has decided to compress the schedule. They have requested extra budget to bring in the additional resources required. Which schedule compression technique are they using?

A. Compressing
B. Crashing
C. Fast tracking
D. Resource leveling

141: You have managed to bring forward the predicted completion date for your project by doing in parallel several of the activities that were scheduled to be done in sequence. This is called what?

A. Crashing
B. Increasing priorities
C. Acceleration
D. Fast tracking

142: You are working on a project to build a new house. Usually you would wait until the concrete foundation dried then erect the wall on top of it. To speed up the project you start putting the wall frame together off site while the concrete foundation is drying. This is an example of which schedule compression technique?

A. Resource leveling
B. Compressing
C. Crashing
D. Fast tracking

143: Your project sponsor asks you to attend a senior management meeting and present a brief update on your project progress. Which of the following would you be best to use in the presentation?

A. Work performance information
B. Project management plan
C. Bar chart
D. Schedule network diagram

144: What is the name of the process that monitors the status of the project to update project progress and manage changes to the schedule baseline?

A. Verify schedule
B. Monitoring and Controlling
C. Control Schedule
D. Develop schedule

145: All of the following are inputs into the Control Schedule process EXCEPT

A. Project schedule
B. Project management plan
C. Work performance information
D. Work performance data

146: Your project schedule performance index (SPI) is 0.9. What does this mean?

A. The amount of buffer in your critical chain methodology is less than optimal
B. The project network diagram was incorrectly put together
C. The project is behind schedule and in need of schedule compression
D. The project is ahead of schedule

147: You are a project manager on a project where your SPI has been calculated at .95. Your earned value (EV) has been calculated at $10,000, and your actual cost (AC) is $10,400, what is your planned value (PV)?

$$SPI = \frac{EV}{PV}$$

0.95   10,000

A. $10,526
B. $10,000
C. $9,500
D. $10,947

148: As part of development of your project schedule you are informed that a particular activity has an estimated optimistic duration of 7 days, an estimated pessimistic duration of 15 days and will most likely take 10 days to complete. Using PERT analysis what is the standard deviation?

A. 1.33
B. 10.33
C. 1.76
D. 0.5

$$\frac{P-O}{6}$$

149: As part of development of your project schedule you are informed that a particular activity has an estimated optimistic duration of 7 days, an estimated pessimistic duration of 15 days and will most likely take 10 days to complete. Your sponsor asks you the activity duration range that you are 95% confident that the activity will be delivered. What is your response?

A. 9 – 11.66 days
B. 8 – 12 days
C. 7.67 – 12.99 days
D. 10 days

$$\pm 2\sigma \text{ from mean}$$

150: Sarah is the project manager for a software project. She and her team are determining the activity duration estimates for the project. She has requested that each team member determine the estimates by multiplying the quantity of work to be performed by the known historical productivity rate of the individual department. Sarah has asked her team to generate the estimates using what technique?

A. Analogous estimating
B. Parametric estimating
C. Three-Point estimating
D. Expert judgment

151: Consider the following information. What is the critical path? Task A has a duration of 3 days and is a starting activity. Task B has a duration of 6 days and has task A as a predecessor. Task C has a duration of 5 days and has tasks A and B as predecessors. Task D has a duration of four days, and has task B as a predecessor. Task E has a duration of one day and has task C as the predecessor. Task F has a duration of six days and has tasks D and E as predecessors. Task G has a duration of four days, and has tasks E and F as predecessors.

A. A-B-C-E-F-G
B. A-D-F-G
C. A-C-D-E-F-G
D. A-B-D-F-G

152: Consider the following information. How many tasks have a slack of 2 days?
Task A has a duration of 3 days and is a starting activity. Task B has a duration of 6 days and has task A as a predecessor. Task C has a duration of 5 days and has tasks A and B as predecessors. Task D has a duration of four days, and has task B as a predecessor. Task E has a duration of one day and has task C as the predecessor. Task F has a duration of six days and has tasks D and E as predecessors. Task G has a duration of four days, and has tasks E and F as predecessors.

A. 1
B. 2
C. 3
D. 4

Project Cost Management

153: You are completing the process of aggregating the estimated costs of individual activities or work packages to establish an authorized cost baseline. What process are you completing?

A. Determine Budget
B. Estimate costs
C. Control costs
D. Cost performance baseline

154: The cost management plan can establish all of the following EXCEPT

A. Units of measure
B. Level of accuracy
C. Activity definition
D. Control thresholds

155: Costs that cannot be directly traced to a specific project and are accumulated and allocated equitably over multiple projects are known as what?

A. Indirect costs
B. Direct costs
C. Allocatable costs
D. Non projectized costs

156: Which of the following is NOT an input into the Estimate Costs process?

A. Project schedule
B. Activity cost estimates
C. Risk register
D. Scope Baseline

157: Which of the following is NOT an organizational process asset you would consider when estimating costs?

A. Lessons learned
B. Cost estimating templates
C. Historical information
D. Market conditions

158: You are estimating the costs in your project and using information from a previous, similar project as the basis for estimating in your current project. What technique are you using?

A. Three point estimating
B. Parametric Estimating
C. Analogous estimating
D. Published estimating data

159: What is the name of the technique for estimating the cost of individual work packages with the lowest level of detail?

A. Low level estimating
B. Parametric estimating
C. Bottom-up estimating
D. Project management software

160: What is the name of the technique that uses a statistical relationship between historical data and other variables to calculate a cost estimate for a schedule activity resource?

A. Statistical estimating
B. Bottom-up estimating
C. Parametric estimating
D. Top-down estimating

161: Which estimating technique is generally less costly than other estimating techniques but also generally less accurate?

A. Parametric estimating
B. Analogous estimating
C. Resource rate estimating
D. Bottom-up estimating

162: While completing the cost estimating process for a particular activity in your project, several members of your team disagree over the estimate to do the work. After discussion with the team you determine that that most likely costs of the activity will be $25, the optimistic cost of the activity will be $15, and the pessimistic cost will be $70. Using the three point estimating technique what is the expected cost of the activity?

A. 36.66
B. 30.83
C. 110
D. 25.83

163: While completing the cost estimating for a particular activity in your project, several members of your team disagree over the estimate to do the work. After discussion with the team you determine that that most likely costs of the activity will be $50, the optimistic cost of the activity will be $30, and the pessimistic cost will be $70. Using the three point estimating technique what is the expected cost of the activity?

A. 50
B. 25
C. 70
D. 150

164: During your cost estimating you include a figure for cost uncertainty on your project. What is this figure generally known as?

A. Contingency reserve
B. Reserve analysis
C. Management reserve
D. Slush fund

165: Your are using the three point estimating method of scheduling for a project you are working on. Using the three point estimating calculation the variance for the project is found to be 16 days and the duration of the project is found to be 90 days. What is the range of values for the project duration such that there will be at least a 95% probability that the actual project completion will fall between the high and low value of the range of values?

A. 58-122 days
B. 74-106 days
C. 82-98 days
D. 86-94 days

166: You are aggregating your cost estimates of individual activities and work packages to establish an authorized cost baseline. What process are you engaged in?

A. Cost performance baseline
B. Budget preparation
C. Estimate costs
D. Determine budget

167: Which of the following is NOT an input into the Determine Budget process?

A. Basis of estimates
B. Cost baseline
C. Activity cost estimates
D. Scope baseline

168: The authorized time-phased budget at completion used to measure, monitor, and control overall cost performance on the project is known as what?

A. Cost baseline
B. Approved project budget
C. Activity cost estimates
D. Total funding requirements

169: You are monitoring the status of the project to update the project budget and managing changes to the cost baseline. What process are you carrying out?

A. Control costs
B. Determine budget
C. Earned value management
D. Cost aggregation

170: All of the following are key elements used in earned value management EXCEPT

A. Work performance information
B. Earned value
C. Planned value
D. Actual cost

171: After measuring your project performance you note that your schedule variance is $75,000. What would your BEST course of action be?

A. Congratulate your project team on doing well with the project but also submit the information through the approved change control process so that any updates required can be made to the schedule baseline documents
B. Ask your project sponsor for extra funds to crash the schedule to catch up time
C. Immediately begin fast tracking the schedule to catch up time
D. Do nothing as everything is going well on your project and you are obviously a good project manager

172: The earned value on your project is $15,000, the planned value is $20,000 and the actual cost is $18,000. What is your schedule variance?

A. 3000
B. 5000
C. -5000
D. -3000

173: The earned value on your project is $18,000, the planned value is $20,000 and the actual cost is $15,000. What is your cost variance?

A. 2000
B. -3000
C. 3000
D. -2000

174: The earned value on your project is $26,000, the planned value is $20,000, and the actual cost is $18,000. What is your schedule variance?

A. 8000
B. 6000
C. -8000
D. 2000

175: The earned value on your project is $52,000, the planned value is $51,000 and the actual cost is $49,000. What is your cost variance?

A. -1000
B. 2000
C. 1000
D. 3000

176: The total planned value for a project is known as what?

A. Budget at completion
B. Cost baseline
C. Actual cost
D. Approved project budget

177: What is the term for the measurement of the authorized work that has been completed and the authorized budget for such completed work?

A. Budget at completion
B. Cost baseline
C. Actual cost
D. Earned value

178: You are a project manager on a large software project using the earned value reporting system to manage your project. At this point in time the EV is $24,000, the BAC is $97,000, the PV is $29,000, and the AC is $45,000. What is the percent complete?

A. 0.53
B. 0.3
C. 0.46
D. 0.25

179: You are working on a large project and have determined that your cost variance (CV) is $50,000 and that your earned value (EV) is $125,000. What is your actual cost (AC)?

A. 50000
B. 75000
C. 175000
D. 125000

180: If you have an actual cost (AC) of $4 500, a planned value (PV) of $5 000, and a Schedule Performance Index (SPI) of 1.1, what is your Cost Performance Index (CPI)?

A. 1.11
B. 0.9
C. 1.22
D. 1.0

181: The earned value on your project is $20000, the actual cost is $18000 and the planned value is $25000. What is your SPI?

A. 1.11
B. 0.8
C. -5000
D. 5000

182: The earned value on your project is $25,000, the actual cost is $20,000 and the planned value is $20,000. What is your SPI?

A. 0.8
B. 0.75
C. 1
D. 1.25

183: The planned value on your project is $120,000, the earned value is $100,000, the actual cost is $90,000 and your cost variance is $10,000. What is your cost performance index?

A. 1.11
B. 3
C. 0.83
D. 1.2

184: The planned value on your project is $9,000, the earned value is $9,000, the actual cost is $8,000 and your cost variance is $1,000. What is your cost performance index?

A. 1.125
B. 1
C. 0.88
D. 8

185: You are working on a large project and have determined that your cost variance (CV) is $50,000 and that your earned value (EV) is $125,000. What is your Cost Performance Index (CPI)?

A. 0.4
B. 1.5
C. 1.666
D. 2.5

186: Your project control measurements show a CPI of 0.89. What does this show about your project?

A. That your project is experiencing a cost overrun for the work completed
B. That your project is only spending 89% of the money need to get 100% of the job done
C. That your project is experiencing a cost underrun for the work completed
D. That your project is running behind schedule and over budget

187: Your project has a CPI of 1.1 and a SPI of .9. What does this mean?

A. You are experiencing a cost underrun and are ahead of schedule
B. You are experiencing a cost overrun and are behind schedule
C. You are experiencing a cost underrun and are behind schedule
D. You are experiencing a cost overrun and are ahead of schedule

188: You are forecasting your estimate to complete your project and are incurring extra costs to do this work. What sort of estimating technique are you using?

A. Bottom-Up EAC estimating
B. Earned value management
C. Estimate to complete forecast
D. To complete performance index

189: Your actual costs on your project are $75,000, the budget at completion is $100,000 and the earned value is $85,000. Your project has experienced some atypical variances to date which have affected its financial performance but from this point forward you expect it to perform at the originally budgeted rate. What is your estimate at completion?

A. $100000
B. $110000
C. $90000
D. $105000

190: Your budget at completion is $50,000, your earned value is $40,000, and your actual cost is $45,000. Using an estimate at completion forecast for ETC work performed at the present CPI what is your estimate at completion?

A. $47666
B. $50000
C. $56818
D. $53225

191: The calculated projection of cost performance that must be achieved on the remaining work to meet a specified management goal such as the BAC or the EAC is known as what?

A. Estimate to complete
B. To-complete performance index
C. Cost baseline
D. Earned value

192: Your actual cost on the project is $10,000, the budget at completion is $20,000, the earned value is $8,000, the cumulative CPI is 0.8 and the cumulative SPI is 0.9. Using both your CPI and SPI factors what is your estimate at completion forecast?

A. $18750
B. $25000
C. $22666
D. $26666

193: Which of the following is NOT an output of the Control Costs process?

A. Change requests
B. Work performance information
C. Cost forecasts
D. Variance analysis

194: You are managing a project and the original scope baseline of the project was budgeted at $100,000. Since work on the project started there have been 13 authorized and approved changes to the project. The changes have a value of $12,000 and the cost of investigating them prior to their approval was $1,500. What is the current budget for the project?

A. $113500
B. $109500
C. $112000
D. $100000

195: The project you are managing is going well and you are using the earned value management system to assess historical information and forecast a likely future financial state of the project. You have a budget at completion of $120,000, earned value of $50,000, planned value of $55,000, and an actual cost of $45,000. What is your To Complete Performance Index (TCPI) to achieve the budget at completion?

A. 1
B. 1.07
C. 0.93
D. $5 000

Project Quality Management

196: Customer satisfaction means that customer requirements are met. Meeting customer requirements requires a combination of what two factors?

A. Continuous improvement and prevention over inspection
B. Conformance to requirements and prevention over inspection
C. Continuous improvement and fitness for use
D. Conformance to requirements and fitness for use

197: In relation to the management of quality on a project FMEA stands for what?

A. Failed measurement and effective assurance
B. Failed measurement and effect analysis
C. Failure mode and effect analysis
D. Failure model of effective analysis

198: Modern quality management complements project management very highly with both disciplines recognizing the importance of all the following characteristics EXCEPT

A. Customer satisfaction
B. Prevention over inspection
C. Continuous improvement
D. Total Quality Management (TQM)

199: Quality is planned, designed and built into your project instead of being inspected in. What is the main reason that prevention of mistakes in quality is preferred over finding the mistakes via inspection?

A. Because your quality management plan focuses on prevention
B. Because if you are a good project manager and perform prevention well you won't have to deal with inspection
C. Because finding defects via inspection should be avoided at all costs
D. Because the cost of preventing mistakes is generally much less than the cost of correcting them when they are found by inspection

200: What is the difference between precision and accuracy?

A. Precision means the degree to which there is conformance to requirements. Accuracy refers to fitness for use
B. Precision means the values of the repeated measurements are clustered and have little scatter. Accuracy means that the measured value is very close to the true value
C. Precision is the degree to which the project quality assurance processes are being met. Accuracy is the degree to which the product meets customer specifications
D. Precision is the ability to provide information to six sigma level. Accuracy is the process of ensuring that the six sigma target is met

201: What is the difference between quality approaches to the project and product?

A. Quality in relation to the project is focused on ensuring the project control and reporting is accurate. Quality in relation to the product ensures that it stays within the upper and lower control limits

B. There is no difference between the two

C. Quality in relation to the project relate to the processes and procedures that run the project. Quality in relation to the product looks at conformance to requirements and fitness of use

D. Quality in relation to the project is focused on the preparation and execution of the quality management plan. Quality in relation to the product is set solely by the customer

202: Your project is behind schedule and you have asked your project team to work longer hours to make up the time so that the customer's needs are met as planned. As project manager you should monitor your quality management plan for what reason?

A. Achieving customer needs is not the primary focus of the quality management plan and you need to make sure your team is working on project quality not product quality at these times

B. The customer requirements and specifications can change rapidly during periods of rework as the customer sees opportunities to make changes

C. Meeting customer requirements by overworking the project team may result in increased employee attrition, errors, or rework

D. The overtime cost incurred will take away project budget assigned to implementation of the quality management plan

203: Your project team has completed a check of the project and the product you are managing. They discover that although you are meeting the quality requirements the product is of a low grade. What should you do FIRST?

A. Check the quality management plan on what to do when discovering a low grade product
B. Keep the project running as normal with no changes as a result of this discovery
C. Immediately stop work and discover the source of the low grade, and proceed to fix it
D. Keep the project running so that you don't lose time, but assign a team member with experience in the area of the product to discover the reason behind the low grade

204: The Japanese developed a method of modern quality management that relies on continuing small improvements involving everyone from the top management to the lowest level worker in the organization. What is this most commonly known as?

A. Kanban
B. Kaizen
C. Kawasaki
D. Kampai

205: The PMBOK® Guide process groups of initiating, planning, executing, monitoring, and controlling a project a based on the work of Shewhart and Deming. What is their quality improvement model known as?

A. Plan-Do-Check-Act Cycle
B. Organizational Project Management Maturity Model (OPM3)
C. Six Sigma
D. Total Quality management (TQM)

206: What does the cost of quality refer to?

A. The amount of money required to complete your project quality management plan

B. The total cost of all efforts related to quality throughout the product life cycle

C. The total cost of the quality effort throughout the project life cycle

D. The total cost of implementing a prevention and inspection regime

207: The process of identifying quality requirements and standards for the project and product is known as what?

A. Perform Quality Assurance

B. Cost of quality

C. Control Quality

D. Plan Quality Management

208: Which of the following is NOT an input into the Plan Quality Management process?

A. Stakeholder register

B. Quality checklists

C. Risk register

D. Requirements documentation

209: Cost of quality includes all of the following characteristics EXCEPT

A. Destructive testing loss

B. Investment in preventing non-conformance to requirements

C. Appraising the product or service for conformance to requirements

D. Failing to meet requirements

210: Which of the following is NOT an example of a cost of conformance?

A. Rework
B. Equipment
C. Training
D. Testing

211: Control charts are used for what purpose?

A. To measure whether the cost of quality is providing the forecast cost benefit analysis
B. To determine if your quality management plan is achieving the objectives
C. To measure if you product is meeting the goal of fitness for use
D. To determine whether or not a process is stable or has predictable performance

212: Control limits for the production rates for the machines your project is building are set at 3 and 9, with a mean value 6 units per hour. The results this week are as follows: 4, 7, 10, 5, and 6. What should you do first?

A. Investigate the third result
B. Continue working
C. Investigate the tenth result
D. Investigate the first result

213: You have received the results of statistical sampling performed on the product of your project. The control chart shows 9 data points in a row just under the mean. What should you do first?

A. Nothing. If the data points are not outside the control limits, then the process is in control.
B. Change the control limits and the mean so the process is under control.
C. Find an assignable or special cause using an Ishikawa diagram.
D. Fire the quality assurance team.

214: Upper and lower control limits are generally set at how many standard deviations above and below the acceptable mean?

A. 1Σ
B. 2Σ
C. 3Σ
D. 6Σ

215: Your project data, as shown on the control chart, indicates the latest seven consecutive points are above the mean but within the upper control limit. What is your BEST course of action?

A. Initiate corrective action in accordance with your quality management plan
B. Do nothing as the data clearly indicates that the process is above the lower specification limit
C. Stop work immediately and investigate the root cause of the problem
D. Lower the lower control limit so that the data is now above the limit

216: Your project is generating useful data for your control chart. The latest data indicates that the process of manufacturing the product has produced units below the lower control limit but above the lower specification limit. What is your BEST course of action?

A. Stop work immediately and investigate the root cause of the problem
B. Do nothing as the data clearly indicates that the process is above the lower specification limit
C. Initiate corrective action in accordance with your quality management plan
D. Lower the lower control limit so that the data is now above the limit

217: During the Plan Quality Management process you are determining the number and type of tests and their impact on cost of quality. What technique are you using?

A. Design of experiments
B. Analogous estimating
C. Benchmarking
D. Cost of Quality

218: You are comparing actual or planned project practices to those of comparable projects to identify best practices and generate ideas for improvement for your project. What quality technique are you using?

A. Analogous estimating
B. Benchmarking
C. Design of experiments
D. Cost of Quality

219: A quality technique that chooses only a part of a population of interest for studying, and is often used to reduce cost, is called what?

A. Inspection
B. Flowcharting
C. Statistical sampling
D. Budget control chart

220: Your project team is working on a software project with over two million lines of code and has just randomly selected a number of lines of code for inspection. What quality technique are they using?

A. Random inspection
B. Design of experiments
C. Benchmarking
D. Statistical sampling

221: Which of the following is NOT an example of a quality planning tool?

A. Affinity diagram
B. Force field diagram
C. Matrix diagrams
D. Quality checklists

222: All of the following are examples of quality metrics EXCEPT

A. Failure rate
B. Budget control
C. Defect frequency
D. Upper control limit

223: Which of the following is NOT an output of the Plan Quality Management process?

A. Quality management plan
B. Quality metrics
C. Process improvement plan
D. Flowcharting

224: The process of continuous process improvements which reduces waste and eliminates activities that do not add value to a project is known as what?

A. Perform quality assurance
B. Plan quality management
C. Control Quality
D. Progressive elaboration

225: All of the following are inputs into the Perform Quality Assurance process EXCEPT

A. Quality audits
B. Process improvement plan
C. Quality metrics
D. Quality control measurements

226: A quality audit is best defined as what?

A. A structured, independent review to determine whether product specifications comply with organizational and project policies, processes and procedures
B. A structured, independent review to determine whether project activities comply with organizational and project policies, processes and procedures
C. An examination of the product specifications to test whether they are fit for use and confirm to requirements
D. A review of the project management plan to ensure it contains the appropriate quality management plan

227: Which of the following is an output of the Perform Quality Assurance process?

A. Quality metrics
B. Change requests
C. Quality audits
D. Process analysis

228: The process of monitoring and recording results of executing the quality activities to assess performance and recommend necessary changes is known as what?

A. Perform quality assurance
B. Control quality
C. Plan quality management
D. Statistical sampling

229: What is the BEST description of the difference between prevention and inspection?

A. Prevention is the systematic adoption of rigorous quality standards during the planning phase. Inspection is carried out during the monitoring and control process group
B. Prevention is concerned with the implementation of the quality process at the start of the project. Inspection is done once the project is underway
C. Prevention is focused on keeping errors out of the process. Inspection is focused on keeping errors out of the hands of the customer
D. Prevention is focused on the quality of the project. Inspection is focused on the quality of the product.

230: What is the BEST description of the difference between tolerances and control limits?

A. Tolerances are concerned with product quality. Control limits are concerned with project quality
B. Tolerances can indicate whether the process is out of control. Control limits specify a range of acceptable results
C. Tolerances are concerned with project quality. Control limits are concerned with product quality
D. Tolerances are a specified range of acceptable results. Control limits are thresholds which can indicate whether the process is out of control

231: All of the following are an example of one of Ishikawa's seven tools of quality EXCEPT

A. Control Charts
B. Flowcharting
C. Run Chart
D. Inspection

232: You are the project manager for a project where quality is an important constraint and are trying to correct a problem with a machine that makes parts that are used in complex medical imaging equipment. As a result of carrying our your Control Quality process you discover that unfortunately these parts are frequently made with defects. You have decided to hold a meeting to discuss the process of making the parts. You create a diagram that has branches that show the possible causes of the problems. Each of the branches breaks the cause down into more and more detail. What is this diagram called?

A. Scatter diagram
B. Fishbowl diagram
C. Pareto diagram
D. Cause and effect diagram

233: You are trying to find the cause of an identified problem on your project by examining the various factors that might be linked to the potential problems. What technique are you using?

A. Control charts
B. Ishikawa diagram
C. Pareto chart
D. Run chart

234: The quality manager on your project wishes to analyze the data that is being received in the form of a list of defects that have occurred in the manufacturing department. The report comes with defects listed chronologically as they occurred, the cost of the repair necessary to correct each defect, the person involved, and a description of the defect. The quality manager would like to determine which of the defects should be corrected first according to the frequency of the defect occurring. Which of the following tools should she use?

A. Quality critical path
B. Sampling inspection
C. Cause and effect diagram
D. Pareto diagram

235: You are explaining to your project team the ranking of causes for defects on your project to enable them to focus their corrective actions on those causes that cause the greatest defects.. What sort of diagram would you use for this?

A. Scatter diagram
B. Pareto chart
C. Control chart
D. Histogram

236: You are using a vertical bar chart to show how often a particular variable state occurred. What is this sort of bar chart more commonly called?

A. Scatter diagram
B. Pareto chart
C. Control chart
D. Histogram

237: You are using a chart similar to a control chart without displayed limits which shows the history and pattern of a variation. What sort of chart are you using?

A. Control charts
B. Run chart
C. Pareto chart
D. Fishbone diagram

238: A visual presentation of data showing the relationship between a dependent and independent variable is known as what?

A. Pareto chart
B. Scatter diagram
C. Control chart
D. Run Chart

239: All of the following are outputs of the Control Quality process EXCEPT

A. Validated changes
B. Quality metrics
C. Change requests
D. Quality control measurements

Project Human Resource Management

240: The processes that organize, recruit, reward, manage and lead the project team are known as what?

A. Project team building and development
B. Project team management
C. Project management
D. Project human resource management

241: The project sponsor has several responsibilities while working with the project management team. Which of the following is not a responsibility of the project sponsor?

A. Project funding
B. Influencing others in support of the project
C. Monitoring progress
D. Completing the WBS

242: What is the generally correct order of activities in the Project Human Resource Management knowledge area?

A. Plan Human Resource Management, Develop Project Team, Acquire Project Team, Manage Project team
B. Develop Project Team, Acquire Project Team, Plan Human Resource Management, Manage Project Team
C. Acquire Project Team, Plan Human Resource Management, Develop Project Team, Manage Project Team
D. Plan Human Resource Management, Acquire Project Team, Develop Project Team, Manage Project Team

243: The Plan Human Resource Management process has a single output, the human resource management plan. This plan is then used as an input into all of the following processes EXCEPT?

A. Identify Risks
B. Estimate Costs
C. Estimate Activity Resources
D. Acquire Project Team

244: All of the following are inputs into the Plan Human Resource Management EXCEPT

A. Enterprise environmental factors
B. Activity resource requirements
C. WBS
D. Organizational process assets

245: You are showing your project team members the organizational structure and point out where in the structure their role is located. What tool would be useful to you in preparing this information?

A. Organizational breakdown structure (OBS)
B. Work breakdown structure (WBS)
C. Resource breakdown structure (RBS)
D. Responsibility assignment matrix (RAM)

246: You are using a matrix based chart to give a clear indication of the connection between work packages and team members. Additionally the chart shows who is responsible, accountable, consulted, and informed about the work. What is the common name of this type of chart?

A. Organizational breakdown structure (OBS)
B. RACI Chart
C. Work breakdown structure (WBS)
D. Responsibility assignment matrix (RAM)

247: As a competent project manager you should be aware of the leading and foundational theories relating to the management of human resources and their practical application. Which of the following is NOT one of these theories?

A. Herzberg's motivation-hygiene theory
B. Maslow's hierarchy of needs
C. McGregor's theory X and theory Y
D. Colbin intuitive behavior modification theory

248: As a competent project manager you should be aware of the leading and foundational theories relating to the management of human resources and their practical application. Which of the following is NOT one of these theories?

A. Vroom's Expectancy Theory
B. Ouchi theory Z
C. McLachlan's theory of external motivation
D. McClelland's Human Motivation, Achievement or Three Needs Theory

249: The human resource management plan can include all the following information EXCEPT

A. Project organization charts
B. Staffing management plan
C. Cost estimates for staff time
D. Roles and responsibilities

250: What does a resource calendar show?

A. The human resource level, constraints and commitment over time
B. The cost of staff members over time
C. The annual leave for staff throughout the project
D. Any programmed team building activities throughout the project

251: You are currently attempting to complete the Acquire Project Team process on a project that is just about to start. You are meeting resistance from the functional managers of the staff you want to use on your project and it appears that you may have to seek help from external consultants. Your project sponsor is concerned about the impact this process is having on the project. All of following are potential adverse effects of not acquiring your project team EXCEPT

A. Decreased customer satisfaction
B. Reduced project costs
C. Reduced quality
D. Delays to project schedules

252: Your construction manager approaches you about a particular team member than has just been assigned to the project. She thinks that they do not have the required skills to complete the work expected of them and suggests that this team member be assigned to a different project. What is your BEST course of action?

A. Arrange for the team member to get the necessary training
B. Tell your construction manager to fire the team member immediately
C. Tell your construction manager that it is ok if the team member learns on the job
D. Arrange for the team member to be assigned to another project

253: You are in the process of obtaining the staff members you require on your project from other functional areas within your organization. You have made a request to a particular functional manager to have one of her staff members assigned part time to your project. The functional manager is concerned about the effect this will have on her operational goals and suggest instead that the staff member be assigned to your project for 30% of their time instead of 50%. What technique are you engaged in?

A. Negotiation
B. Pre-assignment of staff
C. Acquisition
D. Acquire project team

254: The software project you are working on is using developers from different geographic areas around the world because the high level of experience required for this project could not be obtained locally. With the different time zones you are having difficulty organizing regular meetings between all the project team members. What would be the BEST thing you could do to improve communication between your virtual team?

A. Insist they all make themselves available at 10am your time once a week
B. Use real time and recorded web based video conferencing
C. Run multiple meetings on the same topic so that everyone gets the same message
D. Only meet with those team members in your office and tell them to let the other team members know what was discussed

255: What is the process of improving the competencies, team interaction and the overall team environment to enhance project performance known as?

A. Develop Project Team
B. Plan Human Resource Management
C. Acquire Project Team
D. Manage Project Team

256: You are holding a weekly project meeting when a disagreement between two members of the project team begins. The disagreement is over a technical detail of the project. It is important that the conflicting opinions of the two team members be resolved as quickly as possible. It is even more important that the difference of opinion be resolved correctly. What is your BEST course of action?

A. Assign someone to find out more factual information about the problem
B. End the meeting and give everyone a few days to cool off
C. You should make the decision right away to save time and not let the two disagreeing parties stay in disagreement very long
D. You should suggest a compromise between the two disagreeing team members

257: Which of the following is NOT an objective of developing a project team?

A. Get everyone to align themselves with the culture of the project office
B. Improve team members knowledge and skills
C. Improve trust and agreement between team members
D. Create a dynamic and cohesive team culture

258: The Tuckman theory of team development states that team development generally follows a sequence of stages. Which is the correct order of those stages?

A. Performing, Forming, Norming, Storming, Adjourning
B. Storming, Norming, Forming, Performing, Adjourning
C. Forming, Norming, Storming, Performing, Adjourning
D. Forming, Storming, Norming, Performing, Adjourning

259: You have offered your team each an individual financial bonus if they are the first to complete a particular piece of work. Instead of motivating the team your offer has caused unhealthy competition among some staff and apathy amongst others. What could be the problem with your offer?

A. You offered too little money
B. Your team culture does not support individualism
C. You offered too much money
D. Your team do not respect you as project manager

260: Your have decided that all you project team members must move into their own space within the organizations main headquarters to improve efficiency and team building. What is this commonly called?

A. Assignment
B. Project team residential compatibility
C. Co-location
D. War room

261: Which of the following is an output of the Develop Project Team process?

A. Team building activities
B. Team performance assessments
C. Staff assignments
D. WBS dictionary elements

262: As a project manager your greatest challenge has been managing your project team. You have decided to gain extra skills to help you in this task. All of the following are areas you should focus on EXCEPT

A. Negotiation
B. Communication
C. Remuneration
D. Leadership

263: Which of the following is NOT an input into the Manage Project Team process?

A. Project management plan
B. Project staff assignments
C. Project performance appraisals
D. Team performance assessments

264: In his theory of motivation of employees Herzberg divided motivation factors into two classes: satisfiers and dissatisfiers. Examples of satisfiers are

A. Work satisfaction, fringe benefits.
B. Sense of personal achievement, work satisfaction
C. Plush office space, performance-based salary raise
D. Vacation time, assignment of a personal staff assistant

265: As a project manager you understand how important effective management of your team is to the success of the project. Which of the following is NOT a key interpersonal skill that you should have as a manager to help you manage your team?

A. Effective decision making skills
B. The ability to be persuasive and have high levels of active and effective listening skills
C. Strong leadership skills with the ability to communicate the vision and inspire the project team to achieve high performance
D. A focus on prevention over inspection and an eye for detail when reporting your project status reports

266: Your project has been underway for 18 months and currently has a CPI of 1.02 and an SPI of 1.07. During the project two of your project team members have disagreed constantly over non-technical issues and on occasion have shown open hostility towards each other, often in front of other team members. Lately the situation has escalated and during your last project team status meeting they openly shouted at each other. As project manager you decide to call both team members into your office and explain to them that the best way to resolve this conflict is a give and take attitude and open dialogue. What conflict resolution technique are you using?

A. Collaborating and forcing
B. Confronting and problem solving
C. Smoothing and accommodating
D. Withdrawing and avoiding

267: As part of your own professional development plan you have approval from your senior manager to undertake leadership training. As part of your training you have asked your team members for their opinion on what constitutes the key elements and characteristics of an effective leader. What are the key elements of effective leadership?

A. Vision and humor
B. Friendship and admiration
C. Respect and trust
D. Fear and submission

268: Which of the following is not one of the four basic decision making styles normally used by project managers?

A. Command
B. Coin flip
C. Ideas to action
D. Consensus

269: You are faced with a large decision to make on your project. After fully defining the problem, you call in your team to brainstorm multiple solutions. You then define the evaluation criteria and rate the pros and cons of different options. Prior to making a decision you go through a process of problem definition, one solution generation, ideas to action, solution action planning, solution evaluation planning and evaluation of the outcome and process. What process are you using?

A. Six-phase decision making model
B. Shewhart and Deming's Plan-Do-Check-Act cycle
C. Kouzes and Posner 6 step decision making process
D. Turner and Muller's 6-phase decision making process

Project Communications Management

270: All of the following are examples of communication skills EXCEPT

A. Persuading a person or organization to perform an action
B. Setting and managing expectations
C. Reviewing the work breakdown structure to ensure team members know what has to be done
D. Listening actively and effectively

271: What sort of communication is most appropriate when dealing with changes to a contract?

A. Informal written
B. Formal written
C. Formal verbal
D. Electronic

272: After conducting your stakeholder analysis you determine that there are, excluding you, 7 stakeholders on the project. How many communication channels are there?

A. 21
B. 28
C. 7
D. 35

273: There are 12 stakeholders including yourself on the project, how many communication channels are there?

A. 78
B. 144
C. 66
D. 12

274: All of the following are factors which influence the method of communication disbursement between team members EXCEPT

A. Availability of technology
B. Duration of the project
C. Local government regulations
D. Urgency of the need for information

275: You are leading a team on a complex project that requires constant communications with influential stakeholders. Despite your best efforts the message that you send to the stakeholders is disrupted and misunderstood. Communications between the sender and the receiver often are affected by communications barriers or noise. These include all of the following EXCEPT?

A. Cultural differences
B. Differences in motivation
C. Educational differences
D. Lack of a communications device

276: You are having difficulty concentrating on what a stakeholder is saying during a business meeting and you feel you are not fully understanding them. What technique could help you to understand them better?

A. Ask them to write everything down
B. Repeat the message back to the stakeholder
C. Ask to postpone the meeting until you feel better
D. Asking them to speak slower

277: Your project team is scattered over 3 countries in 3 different time zones. Each project office has a different language as its first language and to improve communication you have asked that all correspondence be conducted in English. In doing this what are you trying to minimize in your teams communications?

A. Environmental constraints
B. Cultural differences
C. Noise
D. Foreign accents

278: The skill of listening involves more than just hearing the sounds. One of the characteristics of a good listener is that he or she:

A. Agrees with the speaker
B. Takes good notes
C. Finishes the speaker's sentences
D. Repeats some of the things said

279: You are in the process of sending out your weekly project update to a wide range of stakeholders? This is an example of what sort of communication method?

A. Stakeholder management strategy
B. Pull communication
C. Interactive communication
D. Push communication

280: You are using your intranet site to post large amounts of information that team members can log into to read. This is an example of what sort of communication method?

A. Encoding and decoding
B. Push communication
C. Interactive communication
D. Pull communication

281: Your project team has spent a considerable amount of time and energy completing the stakeholder analysis and putting together the communication management plan but is now disagreeing what, how, and when different communication methods are to be used. Who should take responsibility for determining this?

A. Project sponsor
B. Project team
C. Project manager
D. Stakeholder representative

282: The communication management plan usually provides all the following EXCEPT

A. Stakeholder communication requirements
B. Person responsible for authorizing release of confidential information
C. Glossary of common terminology
D. Team members addresses and phone numbers

283: All of the following are techniques to ensure your project meetings are more productive EXCEPT?

A. Ground rules
B. Teleconferencing
C. Set a start and finish time for the meeting
D. An agenda

284: Effective information distribution includes all the following techniques EXCEPT

A. Writing style
B. Presentation techniques
C. Issue log
D. Choice of media

285: The Manage Communications process occurs within which the PMBOK® Guide process group?

A. Planning
B. Executing
C. Initiating
D. Monitoring and controlling

286: You and your project team have been in negotiations with a potential supplier for several hours over an important contract that will deliver a large part of the one product required to complete your project. You and your team are getting frustrated at the slow rate of progress on the negotiations but know it is important that they are done thoroughly. How important is non-verbal communication to the negotiations?

A. Only important when the other party is silent
B. Not very important
C. Very important
D. Only important during negotiations over cost

287: You have called a team member into your office to deal with unacceptable behavior towards other project team members. After the meeting you decide to follow up to make clear what was discussed. What is the best form of communication to use in this instance?

A. Formal verbal
B. Formal written
C. Informal written
D. Informal verbal

288: There are 36 communications channels on a project. How many stakeholders are there in the project?

A. 9
B. 36
C. 18
D. 6

289: Your project sponsor has asked you to present a detailed project update to some high level stakeholders who are concerned the project is not meeting its agreed timeframes, its agreed budget nor delivering the quality the customer is expecting. What information and method would you be BEST to use in this situation?

A. A PowerPoint presentation outlining the major issues given in your offices
B. A summary milestone report tabled as an agenda item at their next scheduled meeting
C. A detailed performance report in writing with an accompanying presentation and time for questions and answers
D. A verbal presentation during a 10 minute meeting

290: You are attempting to communicate with various project stakeholders and despite your best efforts you find that the information that you send to them is misunderstood. You have fund that cultural differences and using unfamiliar technology are the main problems contributing to this lack of understanding. What is the best term to describe these characteristics?

A. Decoding
B. Feedback
C. Noise
D. Transmission

291: You are actively monitoring and controlling the project communications according to you approved communications management plan and are seeking to generate work performance information about the effectiveness of your project communications. Which of the following would be least useful to you?

A. Issue log
B. Change requests
C. Work performance data
D. Project communications

292: You are using historical data about your project to forecast an estimated future outcome in your project performance reporting. This is an example of what forecasting method?

A. Budget forecasts
B. Judgmental methods
C. Econometric method
D. Time series methods

293: Your project team has just finished the first round of soliciting information from experts about what they think the forecast future performance on your project will be using information supplied to them. You are currently assessing the information supplied anonymously by the respondents and plan to request a second round of opinion to use in your project forecasts. What forecasting method are you using?

A. Earned value
B. Causal method
C. Judgmental method
D. Econometric method

294: Which of the following would you NOT expect to see in a detailed project performance report?

A. Staff performance reviews
B. Current status of risks and issues
C. Forecasted project completion
D. Summary of changes approved in the period

295: Several of your stakeholders are raising issues with you and you are documenting their issues in an issue log and providing feedback to the stakeholders about the status and any resolution of the issues. Furthermore you are using the issue log as an input into a process as it provides a repository for what is already happened in the project and a platform for subsequent communications to be delivered. Which process are you involved in?

A. Plan communications management
B. Manage communications
C. Control communications
D. Monitor and control project work

296: A project manager should spend approximately how much of their time communicating to team members and stakeholder to effectively contribute to project success?

A. 50%
B. 5%
C. 90%
D. 70%

297: Which of the following has been identified as one of the single biggest reasons for project success or failure?

A. The nature of the working relationship between project sponsor and the project manager
B. Financial accountability and accuracy
C. Enterprise environmental factors
D. Appropriate communication

Project Risk Management

298: What is the BEST description of the objectives of risk management?

A. Assess the qualitative and quantitative probability and impact of positive and negative risk to the project
B. Decrease the probability and impact of positive events and increase the probability and impact of negative events
C. Decrease the probability and impact of any risks occurring on the project
D. Increase the probability and impact of positive events and decrease the probability and impact of negative events

299: All of the following are characteristics of risks EXCEPT

A. Is a risk occurs it will have an effect on at least one project objective
B. Risk is an uncertain event or condition
C. Risk cannot be avoided
D. Risk is always in the future

300: When completing your risk management plan you also decide to create a contingency plan. What is the main reason for creating a risk contingency plan?

A. Known risks that if they occur can have a large than anticipated impact on your project
B. To deal with known risks with a large uncertainty about the probability of occurrence
C. Unknown risks that have been identified in the risk management plan
D. Unknown risks which cannot be managed proactively

301: The willingness to accept varying degrees of risk is called what?

A. Risk acceptance
B. Risk tolerance
C. Risk planning
D. Risk analysis

302: When should you begin risk management on a project?

A. Once project planning has commenced
B. As soon as a project is initiated or conceived
C. Once project execution has commenced
D. When you are completing the monitoring and controlling

303: All of the following are inputs into the Plan Risk Management process EXCEPT

A. Stakeholder register
B. Project charter
C. Risk management plan
D. Project management plan

304: You and your project team are currently involved in the process to plan your particular approach to risk management on your project and are using a variety of tools and techniques to assist you to produce the risk management plan. Which of the following is NOT a tool and technique used during the Plan Risk Management process?

A. Analytical techniques
B. Risk probability and impact assessment
C. Expert judgment
D. Meetings

305: As part of your risk management planning you develop a diagram showing the hierarchy of project risks arranged by risk category and subcategory. What is this diagram commonly called?

A. Risk assessment register
B. Risk breakdown structure
C. Probability and impact matrix
D. Risk register

306: Your risk management planning session has produced definitions of risk probability and impact. These are used during what process?

A. Perform qualitative risk analysis
B. Identify risks
C. Perform quantitative risk analysis
D. Plan risk management

307: Your team is carrying out the process of determining which risks may affect the project and documenting their characteristics. You are using a variety of tools and techniques, including documentation reviews, information gathering techniques, checklist analysis, and SWOT analysis. What is the name of this process?

A. Perform qualitative risk analysis
B. Identify risks
C. Perform quantitative risk analysis
D. Plan risk management

308: The output of the Identify Risks process is the risk register. Which of the following processes does NOT use the risk register as an input?

A. Perform Qualitative Risk Analysis
B. Control Risks
C. Plan Procurement Management
D. Estimate Activity Duration

309: You and your team are in the process of identifying all potential uncertainty and risk on your project. You wish to ensure that your risk register is as comprehensive as possible and as such you are looking for as many relevant inputs to assist you in this process as possible. Which of the following is NOT an input into the Identify Risks process?

A. Activity duration estimates
B. Assumptions analysis
C. Stakeholder register
D. Activity cost estimates

310: Which of the following is NOT a tool or technique used in the Identify Risks process?

A. Assumptions analysis
B. Information gathering techniques
C. Risk urgency assessment
D. Delphi technique

311: You and your team are completing the process of identifying risks on your project and you wish to use a particular type of diagram to represent risk characteristics. All of the following are diagramming techniques used during the Identify Risks process EXCEPT

A. Process flow chart
B. Cause and effect diagram
C. Pareto diagram
D. Influence diagram

312: Your initial list of identified risks will generally have all of the following information on it EXCEPT

A. Probability
B. Event
C. Consequence
D. Cause

313: Your team is carrying out the process to identify the risks to the project and is identifying strengths and weaknesses of the organization the looking at the way these strengths offset threats and opportunities that may serve to overcome weaknesses. What technique are they using?

A. SWOT analysis
B. Expert judgment
C. PERT analysis
D. PEST analysis

314: As project manager on a project you have begun the process of qualitatively assessing the probability and impact to identified risks that have been identified on your project. Which of the following is NOT an input into the Perform Qualitative Risk Analysis process?

A. Risk register
B. Risk management plan
C. Project charter
D. Scope baseline

315: Your team is using the project risk register and has started a quantitative assessment of the risks. You tell your team that it is better to start with qualitative analysis first. What reasons do you give your team for this decision?

A. Quantitative analysis takes the numerical values assigned during the qualitative process and adds a more intuitive interpretation of the risks
B. Qualitative analysis provides accurate numerical values based on probability and impact that can then be quantified
C. There is no particular reason why one should be done before the other. It is just the way your organizational processes require the process to be completed
D. Qualitative analysis provides a subjective and rapid means of prioritizing risks, and indicating which risk can have quantitative analysis applied to them

316: Your team is using your risk register to prioritize risks for further analysis by assessing their probability of occurrence and impact. What process are they carrying out?

A. Perform Qualitative Risk Analysis
B. Perform Quantitative Risk Analysis
C. Identify Risks
D. Plan Risk Management

317: While completing your assessment of the risks on your project you begin to examine the ones with the greatest potential threat to your project. You are using a diagram to help you complete this task and currently looking at the high priority risks for further analysis. What diagram would best help you?

A. Probability and impact matrix
B. Scatter diagram
C. Pareto chart
D. Risk register

318: An important aspect of your qualitative risk analysis is determining the validity of the information you are using. What is this technique commonly called?

A. Assumption analysis
B. Risk data quality assessment
C. Risk urgency assessment
D. Risk categorization

319: Your team is completing the process of numerically analyzing the effect of identified risks on your project objectives. What process are they carrying out?

A. Plan Risk Response
B. Perform Qualitative Risk Analysis
C. Perform Quantitative Risk Analysis
D. Identify Risks

320: The output of the Perform Quantitative Risk Analysis process is risk register updates. Which process uses this as an input?

A. Project Integration Management
B. Identify risks
C. Project Time Management
D. Plan Risk Responses

321: Three point estimating is a commonly used technique for gathering and analyzing data. It is commonly used as a tool or technique in all of the following project areas EXCEPT

A. Project Quality Management
B. Project Time Management
C. Project Risk Management
D. Project Cost Management

322: If a project has a 40 percent chance of achieving a $17,000 profit and a 60 percent chance of achieving a $20,000 loss, what is the expected monetary value of the project?

A. -5200
B. 37000
C. 5200
D. -3000

323: If a project has a 65 percent chance of a $200,000 profit and a 35 percent chance of a $100,000 loss, what is the expected monetary value for the project?

A. 165000
B. 100000
C. 95000
D. -100000

324: If a risk event has a 80 percent chance of occurring and if it does occur the consequences will be a $10,000 cost to the project. What does -$8,000 represent to the project?

A. Expected monetary value
B. Probabilistic risk assessment
C. What if analysis result
D. Quantified risk

325: After completing your risk register and a quantitative assessment of the financial value of prioritized risks on your project you have a dollar amount added to your project budget. What is this amount typically called?

A. Contingent response strategy
B. Management reserve
C. Slush fund
D. Contingency reserve

326: Which of the following is NOT an example of a probability distribution?

A. Obtuse distribution
B. Normal distribution
C. Triangular distribution
D. Beta distribution

327: Your team is completing an exercise to determine which risks have the greatest potential impact on your project. They are assessing the extent to which the uncertainty of each element of the project effects the risk being examined when all other uncertain elements are held at static baseline values. What is this technique commonly known as?

A. Sensitivity analysis
B. Expected monetary value analysis
C. Tornado diagram
D. Modeling and simulation

328: You are currently performing risk analysis on a large and extremely complex project. Your project team decides that the most comprehensive way to approach the process of risk analysis is to examine all the possible outcomes using an iterative computer simulation process to model a range of variables taken from a probability distribution. What is this technique known as?

A. Sensitivity analysis
B. Expected monetary value analysis
C. Monte Carlo analysis
D. Ishikawa analysis

329: You have documented and quantitatively assessed the risk to your projects and the potential outcomes in a diagram to show the different outcomes of events should a particular probability occur to determine the expected monetary value. What is this technique generally called?

A. Decision tree analysis
B. What-if scenario analysis
C. Ishikawa diagram
D. Tornado diagram

330: Your team has completed the process of assessing and documenting risks that may occur on your project. What is the next step to complete?

A. Identify risks
B. Control Risks
C. Plan risk responses
D. Execute the project tasks

331: A project manager is faced with making a large decision about a risk that her project team has identified. The risk involves the design of a car component. It has been found that the weld of the component where the load bearing flange is located will corrode in a high salt environment. If this takes place the component may fail and injure the driver and passenger. The project team decides that the design of the component should be modified by using corrosion resistant materials. This will eliminate the risk from consideration. This risk response technique is called:

A. Risk acceptance
B. Risk avoidance
C. Risk rejection
D. Risk transference

332: You are managing a project to build a large hydro dam for electrical power generation which will be built over a known seismically active area. Your team decides to strengthen the core structure of the dam to better tolerate any earth movements that may occur. This is an example of what sort of risk response?

A. Avoid
B. Transfer
C. Mitigate
D. Accept

333: You have decided to take out insurance on your project to cover your project financially if a risk occurs. This is an example of what sort of risk response?

A. Avoidance
B. Mitigation
C. Sharing
D. Transference

334: All of the following are acceptable responses to positive risks EXCEPT

A. Exploit
B. Accept
C. Enhance
D. Mitigate

335: You are about to tender for a large multi-billion dollar infrastructure project and your general manager has just announced a joint venture with another company to help with risk management. This is an example of what sort of risk response?

A. Sharing
B. Avoidance
C. Mitigation
D. Exploiting

336: You in your project team have completed your risk register, including planned responses to identified risks. What is your next step?

A. Update the work breakdown structure
B. Begin the Control Risks process
C. Perform another iteration of the risk register
D. Update your project sponsor on the plan risk responses

337: All of the following are outputs from the Plan Risk Responses process EXCEPT

A. Project document updates
B. Project management plan updates
C. Updates to the cost management plan
D. Contingent response strategies

338: Your project has been underway for 9 months when a major problem occurs that is not included in the risk register. What is your BEST course of action?

A. Begin the process of evaluating the risk quantitatively then qualitatively
B. Create a workaround
C. Begin the process of evaluating the risk qualitatively then quantitatively
D. Contact your project sponsor

339: Despite your best efforts at anticipating and documenting all risk and uncertainty on your project you have encountered a completely unforeseeable risk that will incur significant extra cost to your project. You decide to approach your project sponsor and ask for permission to get these extra funds from a pool of money that they control. What is this pool of money generally referred to as?

A. Management reserve
B. Contingency reserve
C. Slush fund
D. Control account

340: The project you are working on is over halfway through and you have begun to measure that price increases on the steel that you require for the project have gone 2% over your estimate for price increases over the timeframe of the project. As a result you put in place a policy to procure all the remaining steel require for the project and pay for it to be stored in a warehouse instead of ordering the steel as you require it. This is an example of what?

A. Exploiting
B. Mitigation
C. Transference
D. Contingent response strategy

341: All of the following are inputs into the Control Risks process EXCEPT

A. Project management plan
B. Quality control measurements
C. Work performance reports
D. Risk register

342: You are conducting the process of implementing your risk response plans, tracking identified risks, monitoring residual risks, and identifying new risks? What is this process called?

A. Control Risks
B. Risk Management
C. Risk Assessment
D. Assess and Control Risks

343: During your regular monitoring of the risks identified on your project you examine and document the effectiveness of risk responses in dealing with identified risks and their root causes. What technique are you using?

A. Risk audits
B. Ishikawa analysis
C. Risk urgency assessment
D. Trend analysis

344: All of the following are outputs of the Control Risks process EXCEPT

A. Work performance data
B. Change requests
C. Organizational process assets updates
D. Project management plan updates

Project Procurement Management

345: During the process of procurement management the organization you work for can be all of the following EXCEPT

A. Buyer of products
B. Seller of services
C. Buyer and seller of products or services
D. Insolvent

346: What is the generally accepted correct sequence of processes in the Project Procurement Management knowledge area?

A. Plan Procurement Management, Conduct Procurements, Close Procurements, Control Procurements
B. Conduct Procurements, Plan Procurement Management, Control Procurements, Close Procurements
C. Plan Procurement Management, Conduct Procurements, Control Procurements, Close Procurements
D. Plan Procurement Management, Control Procurements, Conduct Procurements, Close Procurements

347: You are carrying out the contract management and change control processes required to develop and administer contracts for you project. What is this commonly referred to?

A. Plan Procurement Management
B. Close Procurements
C. Project Integration Management
D. Project Procurement Management

348: All of the following are examples of legally binding agreements EXCEPT

A. Subcontract
B. Organizational process assets
C. Agreement
D. Purchase order

349: You are just about to begin the process of procuring services from external providers and you think there may be a standard set of rules governing this process. Where would you be BEST to look for these rules?

A. Ask your organizations legal team
B. Lessons learned
C. The PMBOK® Guide
D. Organizational process assets

350: You have completed the work described in the contract as per the required specifications but the customer is complaining that the product is not what they wanted. What is your BEST course of action?

A. Ask your project sponsor to clarify the scope of the project
B. Restart the project and complete the work the way the customer wants it
C. Ask the customer to note down their concerns in writing and present them to you project team at the next team meeting
D. Enter the Close Procurements process

351: Which of the following is NOT a term used to describe the buyer in a contract?

A. Entrepreneur
B. Client
C. Service requestor
D. Prime contractor

352: Which of the following is NOT a term used to describe the seller in a contract?

A. Vendor
B. Dealer
C. Service provider
D. Contractor

353: You in your project team are completing the process of producing your procurement management plan and want to make sure that you have completed a robust process and used all the possible and appropriate inputs. Which of the following is NOT an input into the Plan Procurement Management process?

A. Activity resource requirements
B. Make-or-buy decisions
C. Stakeholder register
D. Requirements documentation

354: You are carrying out the procurement of services necessary for your project. After consulting with your organizational process assets, specifically the procurement guidelines, which specify that you are to use the most commonly used contract type, you offer the seller what type of contract?

A. Cost plus incentive Fee
B. Time and materials
C. Fixed price incentive fee
D. Firm fixed price

355: You discover that there is a part of the project that contains some risk. Your strategy to deal with this risk is to subcontract the work to an outside supplier by using a firm fixed-price contract. Which of the following must you do?

A. You should make certain that the project team does not reveal the risk to the supplier until the contract is signed
B. You should make every effort to make sure that the supplier is made aware of the risk after the contract is signed
C. You should make sure that the supplier understands the risk before the contract is signed
D. You should assign a member of the project team to monitor the activity of the supplier to make sure that the supplier deals with the risk properly if it occurs

356: You are the project manager for a project that is well underway using a contractor that has agreed to work on a fixed price contract on the project that calls for a single, lump sum payment upon completion of the contract. The contractor's project manager contacts you and informs you that cashflow problems are making it difficult for the contractor to pay employees and subcontractors. The contractor then asks you for a partial payment for work accomplished to date. What is your best course of action?

A. Make no payments to the contractor until all the work is completed as per the terms of the agreed contract
B. Negotiate a change to the contract to allow payments to the contractor
C. Paying for work accomplished to date
D. Starting to make partial payments to the contractor

357: Your organization is providing services to another organization as part of a project. What of the following contract types would your organization prefer to engage in to carry out the work?

A. Fixed price with economic price adjustment
B. Cost plus incentive Fee
C. Firm fixed price
D. Fixed price incentive fee contract

358: Your project has begun with a planned series of iterations that will gradually define the scope of work required. You are negotiating with a potential supplier of services. What is the BEST form of contract to enter into?

A. Fixed price incentive fee
B. Time and materials
C. Cost plus fixed fee
D. Firm fixed price

359: During your project there has been an unforeseen amount of work that requires urgent and immediate attention from an external contractor to ensure it does not adversely affect the project. What sort of contract for services is BEST to use in this instance?

A. Time and materials
B. Fixed price incentive fee
C. Cost plus fixed fee
D. Cost plus incentive fee

360: You are leading your team through the process of making procurement decisions, and selecting the appropriate procurement documentation to use when procuring services from external contractors. Which of the following is not a form of procurement document?

A. Request for proposal (RFP)
B. Request for fixed price contract (RFPC)
C. Request for quotation (RFQ)
D. Request for information (RFI)

361: Which of the following is NOT an output of the Plan Procurement Management process?

A. Source selection criteria
B. Procurement statement of work
C. Procurement management plan
D. Project scope statement

362: You are the project manager on a large project to develop a new customer information database for your organization. You are currently assessing the merits of developing key components of the required software in-house by your own development team compared to getting an external contractor to complete the work. What technique are you using?

A. Expert judgment
B. Risk related contract decisions
C. Source selection criteria
D. Make-or-buy analysis

363: You are leaving your project team to analyze responses received some of your procurement documents and you are beginning the process of selecting the successful seller. Which of the following is NOT an example of selection criteria used to select sellers?

A. Make-or-buy decision
B. Technical capability
C. Management approach
D. Proprietary rights

364: You are currently obtaining seller responses to an RFP you issued and after assessing the responses you expect to select a seller and award a contract for delivery for services on your project. What process are you carrying out?

A. Close Procurements
B. Plan Procurement Management
C. Conduct Procurements
D. Control Procurements

365: You are carrying out the process of obtaining seller responses, selecting seller, an awarding a contract. You wish to make sure that you complete the process of thoroughly and use any and all inputs which may be useful to you. Which of the following is NOT an input into the Conduct Procurements process?

A. Project management plan
B. Source selection criteria
C. Procurement statement of work
D. Resource calendars

366: You have just finished preparation of an exhaustive RFP for you project and are about to send it out to potential service providers. Based on past acceptable performance you decide to send the RFP to a small group of potential suppliers and not all the suppliers who may be interested in providing a response. What technique are you using?

A. Bidder conference
B. Qualified seller list
C. Procurement management plan
D. Proposal evaluation technique

367: After soliciting responses from prospective sellers you are in the process of considering each seller's response against a set of criteria in order to determine who will be the seller selected to provide the required services. The process is giving a greater weight to previous experience in this type of work than it is giving to the price submitted. What technique are you using?

A. Procurement negotiations
B. Weighted average calculation
C. Expert judgment
D. Weighted criteria

368: You are carrying out a bidder conference which is attended by 5 potential sellers of services to your project. You have spent considerable amount of time explaining the statement of work and answering questions from the sellers at the bidder conference. During a break in the afternoon one of the sellers approaches you and asks a question relating to the statement of work. What is your BEST course of action?

A. Explain to the seller that they should wait until the session begins again and then submit their question
B. Refuse to provide an answer to the seller
C. Provide an answer to the seller
D. Ask the seller to leave the room and remove them from the process

369: You are in the process of ensuring that the seller you have engaged to provide a product for your project is meeting the contractual requirements expected of them. What process are you carrying out?

A. Conduct Procurements
B. Control Procurements
C. Close Procurements
D. Plan Procurement Management

370: As part of your project you are looking to make sure that you complete the control procurements process properly in order to ensure that you are managing procurement relationships, monitoring contract performance, and making changes and corrections to contracts as appropriate. As part of this process you want to make sure that you are using all the appropriate inputs. Which of the following processes does not provide an input into the Control Procurements process?

A. Direct and Manage Project Work
B. Monitor and control project work
C. Perform Integrated Change Control
D. Control costs

371: As part of your project you are looking to make sure that you complete the control procurements process properly in order to ensure that you are managing procurement relationships, monitoring contract performance, and making changes and corrections to contracts as appropriate. In order to do this process thoroughly you have decided to review all the possible tools and techniques that you could use. All of the following are tools or techniques used in the Control Procurements process EXCEPT?

A. Inspections and audits
B. Performance reporting
C. Work Performance Information
D. Claims administration

372: You are the project manager on a large project that has been underway for 5 years. You project has consistently reported a CPI of 1.2 and an SPI of 1.3. Delivery of the expected product of the project has been in accordance with the customers expectations and you are beginning the process of closing the project. Your project team is confused about whether to complete the Close Procurements process or the Close Project process first. What is your BEST advice to your project team?

A. It does not matter which order they are completed in as long as they are both completed according to the organizations project management guidelines
B. Only complete the Close Project process as it incorporates the Close Procurements process
C. Complete the Close Project process first then the Close Procurements process so that any final payments incurred by the Close Project process can be made
D. Complete the Close Procurements process first as the contracts need to be closed before the project can be closed by the Close Project process

373: You and your project team are completing the work required by contract with a buyer when your general manager decides to suddenly terminate the contract due to factors that are outside of your control. What is your BEST course of action?

A. Explain to your manager that you are contractually bound to carry out the work
B. Contact the buyer and explain the situation to them
C. Review the WBS for errors in the scope of work
D. Begin the Close Procurements process

374: As part of closing out all the contracts you have used on the project you are wanting to make sure that you demonstrate to your team what is considered best practice in this area and have available to you all potential, tools and techniques that could assist. Which of the following is NOT a tool or technique used in the Close Procurements process?

A. Procurement audits
B. Procurement negotiations
C. Bidder conferences
D. Records management system

375: You are completing the Close Procurements process and are informing sellers that the contract has been completed. What is the BEST way to do this?

A. At the completion party
B. In person
C. Via email
D. By written letter

376: You have entered into an agreement with a seller to provide the goods you require for your project. You have selected to use a fixed-price incentive fee form of contract with a target cost of $100,000, a target price of $120,000, a ceiling price of $140,000, with a sharing ratio of 80/20 to the buyer. What is your point of total assumption?

A. $120,000
B. $140,000
C. $125,000
D. $130,000

Project Stakeholder Management

377: All of the following are stakeholder attributes you should analyze as part of the process to identify stakeholders EXCEPT

A. Their personal conflict resolution style
B. Their expectations of the project
C. Their influence on the project
D. Their interest in the project

378: Which of the following is NOT an input into the Identify Stakeholders process?

A. Procurement documents
B. Project charter
C. Stakeholder register
D. Lessons learned

379: With the help of your project team you are busy identifying all potential project stakeholders and information about them. You are then interviewing all the stakeholders you have identified in an effort to learn more about their interaction with your project and also to gain knowledge of any other stakeholders you may not be aware of. After completing this process you then identify the potential impact or support each stakeholder could generate. Finally you assess how the key stakeholders are likely to react in various situations so you can plan for this. What are you carrying out?

A. Stakeholder management strategy
B. Stakeholder analysis
C. Stakeholder register assimilation
D. Stakeholder communications analysis

380: You are showing your team the relative interest and power each identified stakeholder has in your project. What is the BEST way to show this information?

A. Stakeholder register template
B. Control chart
C. Power/Interest Grid
D. Salience model

381: You have just taken over a project that has been underway for 8 months. The project is performing well and is currently reporting a CPI of 1.2 and an EAC of $1.2m. As part of your familiarization process you want to understand who the stakeholders on the project are. Where would you find this information?

A. Email distribution list
B. Organizational process assets
C. Stakeholder management strategy
D. Stakeholder register

382: You have just taken over a project that is nearing the end of its lifecycle. Shortly after taking control of the project you note that a particular stakeholder is having a negative impact upon the project. You decide that this presents an unacceptable risk to the project and look for a way to manage the stakeholder. Which document will you look for?

A. Stakeholder register
B. Stakeholder analysis
C. Stakeholder analysis matrix
D. Stakeholder management appropriation register

383: An output of the Plan Communications Management process is the communications management plan. This is used as an input into which of the following processes?

A. Plan quality management
B. Manage stakeholder engagement
C. Estimate costs
D. Close project or phase

384: You are completing the process of communication and working with stakeholders to meet their needs and addressing issues as they occur. Which process are you completing?

A. Manage stakeholder engagement
B. Manage Communications
C. Stakeholder analysis
D. Control communications

385: Your project is half way through its expected duration and has a CPI of 1.3 and an SPI of 1.2. Your project sponsor has told you during a meeting that in her eyes the project is a failure because of the feedback she has been getting from important stakeholders on the project. You are surprised at this as the project is performing well financially and is ahead of schedule and you are sure the quality of the work you are completing is of a high standard and meets customer requirements. As the meeting closes your project sponsor asks what you intend to do about the situation? Your BEST response would be what?

A. Send out an email to all stakeholders telling them how great the project is performing financially and time wise
B. Quit the project
C. Say nothing
D. Revisit the manage stakeholder expectation process in your communications management plan

386: What is your primary goal in managing and identifying stakeholders expectations?

A. Your primary goal in identifying and managing stakeholder expectations is to be able to contact stakeholders when you need to send project communications.
B. Your primary goal, and identifying and managing stakeholder expectations is to either get stakeholders to support your project or at least not to oppose it.
C. Your primary goal in identifying and managing stakeholder expectations is to be able to introduce key stakeholders to each other so they can exchange project information.
D. Your primary goal in identifying and managing stakeholder expectations is to be able to determine which of the stakeholders can be most easily influenced and which will require a greater amount of effort.

387: You and your project team are systematically gathering and analyzing quantitative and qualitative information to determine which stakeholders interests should be taken into account throughout the project. You have identified the interests, expectations, and influence of individual stakeholders and related them to the purpose of the project. What tool or technique are you using?

A. Stakeholder analysis
B. Expert judgment
C. Information gathering techniques
D. Meetings

388: You are using a classification model for stakeholder analysis, that describes classes of stakeholders based on their power, urgency, and legitimacy. What is the name of this particular model stakeholder analysis?

A. Power/interest grid
B. Salience model
C. Influence/impact grid
D. Pareto chart

389: As part of your analysis of stakeholder engagement you have classified each stakeholders as either being unaware, resistant, neutral, supportive, or leading when it comes to the level of their engagement with the project. This is an example of what sort of technique?

A. Analytical techniques
B. Information gathering techniques
C. Stakeholder analysis
D. Expert judgment

390: As a senior project manager on a complex project with many stakeholders you are consistently having to coordinate and harmonize stakeholders towards supporting the project and accomplishing the project objectives. In order to do this you are using your skills and facilitating consensus, and influencing people, negotiating agreements and modifying organizational behavior to accept the project outcomes. These are examples of what?

A. Management skills
B. Interpersonal skills
C. Communication methods
D. Information gathering techniques

391: You are managing a complex project with many stakeholders each with their own interest in the project. You have begun the process of monitoring overall project stakeholder relationships and adjusting your stakeholder expectation management strategies and plans were engaging stakeholders to suit the changing project circumstances. Your goal is to increase the efficiency and effectiveness of stakeholder engagement activity. What process are you are engaged in?

A. Manage stakeholder engagement
B. Control stakeholder engagement
C. Control communications
D. Manage communications

392: As a result of controlling stakeholder engagement on your project you are generating a number of organizational process assets updates relating to monitoring overall project stakeholder relationships, their level of engagement and satisfaction with your project. Which of the following is not an organizational process asset that would be updated as a result of this process?

A. Project presentations
B. Project records
C. Issue log
D. Stakeholder notifications

Ethics and Professional Conduct

393: A colleague of yours who was your mentor in your earlier career still claims to have the PMP® credential when you are aware that it has expired several years ago. What should you do FIRST?

A. Let your manager know and let them deal with it
B. Report your colleague to PMI
C. Approach your colleague and ask them to remove any reference to the credential
D. Do nothing as it does not affect your colleague's work performance

394: A project is nearing the end and is reporting a CPI of 1.01, and a SPI of 1.3. The project manager who managed it has been reassigned to another more urgent project and you have been brought in to close the project. While reviewing the financial accounts for the project you discover that the previous project manager made a large payment that was not approved in accordance with the policies of your company. What is the BEST thing you can do?

A. Do nothing as the project has come in under budget
B. Notify the project sponsor
C. Confront the previous project manager and ask them to explain
D. Carry on as if nothing had happened

395: The project administrator working for you on the project does not have the level of skills you assumed he had. What is your BEST course of action?

A. Assign him lower level tasks and bring in another more qualified person
B. Do nothing, he will learn on the job
C. Assign the project administrator to another project
D. Organize training for him

396: You and your project administrator have been working on a detailed project progress report to present to high level stakeholders. You leave it up to the project administrator to complete the report and he emails it to you on the day of the meeting. You are having a busy day and don't get a chance to read the report but as you walk into the meeting you notice some large errors in the financial reporting section of the report? What is your BEST course of action?

A. Reschedule the meeting for another time to give you the chance to fix the errors
B. Give the report to the stakeholders and point out the project administrators errors
C. Give the report in the meeting and accept the blame personally for any errors
D. Get the project administrator to appear before the stakeholders to explain the mistakes

397: You are completing a large infrastructure project in a foreign country. The government officials of the country are extremely grateful for the work you are doing and one of them sends a large cash payment to you to thank you and your team for the work they have done. What should you do?

A. Ask the government official if you can have a car instead of cash
B. Accept the payment and divide it up among team members
C. Gratefully accept the payment and send a thank you card to the donor
D. Refuse the payment

398: You are currently preparing monthly status reports for you project and you are planning on reporting that the project has an SPI of 1.02 and a CPI of .83. Your project sponsor approaches you and says that she has been given a directive by the CEO of the company to report only positive figures or else he is afraid the shareholders in the company will demand changes to the organization. You are confident that the next month's status report will show a CPI greater than one. What should you do?

A. Report the CPI based on what you believe next months figures will be
B. Explain to your project sponsor the reasons why you believe the project reporting should be honest
C. Resign from the project
D. Report the project sponsors behavior to the CEO

399: You are the project manager for a large project that has been completed on time and on budget. The customer and all of the stakeholders are very pleased with the results. As a direct result of the successful completion of the project, your project sponsor approves a bonus of $10,000 to you. There are twelve members on your project team. However, one of the people on the project team has been a very low contributor to the project; the other eleven have all been above standard. What should you do with the money?

A. Divide the money equally among all the team members
B. Ask the team members how they would divide the money
C. Keep the money yourself; you deserve it, and the manager gave it to you
D. Divide the money equally among the team members except for the substandard team member

400: You are the project manager for a large software implementation project that is nearing completion when you discover that one of your technicians has been taking shortcuts with the code being written and it is below the standard required in the technical specification. You and a senior team member review the code used and form the opinion that it will probably not affect the functionality of the final software product. What is your NEXT course of action?

A. Carry on as planned and submit a change request
B. Stop the project and start again, this time writing the code as per the specification
C. Record the discrepancy, inform the customer and look for ways to ensure the project won't be affected
D. Ignore the problem

401: You are the project manager for a project that has high visibility and your project sponsor wants you to prepare a presentation for her to present at a conference. Most of the material in the presentation will be facts that are the results of your project. Your sponsor intends to present the material under her own name and your name will not appear. What is your BEST course of action?

A. Present your own presentation
B. Do the work as you were told by your manager
C. Explain to the sponsor that the correct thing to do is to acknowledge all authors and contributors to the work and, if necessary refuse to work on the presentation unless you are listed as a co-author
D. Meet with your project sponsors manager and discuss the problem

402: You are working in a foreign country delivering a reconstruction project after a large natural disaster. It is normal in this country for government officials to request bribes to assist with processing the consents you require. During a meeting with a government official he mentions that if you pay a $500 bribe you can have the consent you require tomorrow. What is your BEST course of action?

A. Report the official to his manager
B. Pay the $500 out of your own pocket
C. Ask the official for an invoice so the payment can be made by the project
D. Refuse to pay the bribe

403: You are working on a project to construct a new water treatment plant and are waiting on consents required from the government before you can proceed with the work. During a meeting with a government employee to discuss the required consent the employee mentions that the consent can be processed faster if you are willing to pay a processing fee. What is your BEST course of action?

A. Pay the fee if your project budget has allowed for it
B. Explain that you are not permitted to pay bribes
C. Walk out of the meeting and notify your project sponsor
D. Ask the employee if he will accept goods instead of cash so you can hide the transaction better

404: You have just completed the selection of a preferred seller for an upcoming project and have scheduled a meeting in two days time to finalize the contract when your manager informs you that due to current economic conditions that project will now probably not be going ahead and the definite answer will be provided by the CEO in 3 days time. What is your BEST course of action?

A. Postpone the meeting until the fate of the project is clear
B. Go ahead with the meeting, complete the negotiations knowing you can use the termination clauses to end it
C. Go ahead with the meeting, but make an excuse to not sign the contract
D. Cancel the meeting and let the other party know why

Answers

1: The correct answer is B

A. The promotion of the profession of project management is part of your professional responsibilities and using internationally recognized and standardized publications like the PMBOK® Guide is an example of this.
B. The promotion of the profession of project management is part of your professional responsibilities and using internationally recognized and standardized publications like the PMBOK® Guide is an example of this.
C. The promotion of the profession of project management is part of your professional responsibilities and using internationally recognized and standardized publications like the PMBOK® Guide is an example of this.
D. The promotion of the profession of project management is part of your professional responsibilities and using internationally recognized and standardized publications like the PMBOK® Guide is an example of this.

2: The correct answer is A

A. The project doesn't end simply because the project manager resigns. In this instance a new project manager would be recruited and the project would continue.
B. If the project objectives have been achieved then the project would end as there is no longer a need to continue the project.
C. If a project is terminated for any reason it will be considered to be ended.
D. If the need for the project no longer exists then the project would end.

3: The correct answer is D

A. This answer is not correct because it describes operational work which is repetitive and ongoing
B. This answer is not correct because there are projects and operational activities that are both constrained by finances and time. It must also have a unique product, service or result to be a project
C. This answer is not correct because it does not refer to the temporal nature to the work being completed

D. A project is differentiated from operational activity by the fact that it is designed to deliver a unique product within a specified time period where as operational work is ongoing and repetitive.

4: The correct answer is B

A. Building a new house is an example of a project because it has a defined time and delivers a unique product service or result.
B. Achieving 3% growth on last year's sales figures is an operational goal in line with on-going repetitive company activity and as such it is not an example of a project.
C. Designing a new software solution is an example of a project because it has a defined beginning and end and a unique deliverable.
D. Implementing a new business process is an example of a project because it has a defined beginning and end and a unique deliverable.

5: The correct answer is D

A. Executing is one of the 5 PMBOK® guide process groups.
B. Closing is one of the 5 PMBOK® guide process groups.
C. Initiating is one of the 5 PMBOK® guide process groups.
D. Checking is not the correct answer because it is not the right term. You may have thought this described the monitoring and controlling process.

6: The correct answer is D

A. Risks is not correct because risks refer to any areas of positive or negative uncertainty on the project.
B. Opportunities is not correct because opportunities are the opposite of constraints.
C. Constrictions is not correct because the correct terminology is constraint not constriction.
D. Constraints is correct because central to any successful project management is an awareness that a project manager must balance competing constraints on the project. A change in one area can and usually does also mean a potential change in another area.

7: The correct answer is B

A. Project life cycle is not correct as it refers to the entire project life cycle which it subject to progressive elaboration.

B. Progressive elaboration is correct because very rarely will you ever encounter a project where every detail is known at the beginning of a project and there are no changes to the project. It is typical for a project management plan to be iterative in response to this potential for change. The process of knowing more detail as the project develops is known as progressive elaboration.

C. Continuous improvement is not correct as continuous improvement is a concept from project quality management processes that seeks to improve all aspects of project quality.

D. Iterative expectation management is not correct as it is not a term referenced within the PMBOK® Guide.

8: The correct answer is C

A. A group of related projects managed in a coordinated way is not correct because a group of projects managed in a related way is referred to as a program.

B. A group of projects managed by a project director is not correct as a project director can manage projects, programs or portfolios.

C. This answer is correct because portfolio management is typically used by more mature companies to align projects with their strategic aspirations in order to increase the chances of project success and of meeting strategic goals.

D. A collection of projects relating to a single business unit within an organization is not correct as they may be managed as individual projects or a program.

9: The correct answer is B

A. Portfolio is not correct because a portfolio describes all projects that an organization is undertaking and they may or may not be related in some way.

B. Program is correct because a program is a group of projects that are interrelated in someway. A project may be part of a program, but a program will always have projects.

C. PMO is incorrect because a Project Management Office (PMO) describes the center for excellence in project management for an organization.

D. Life Cycle is not correct because a life cycle is a concept describing either a project or product from inception to completion.

10: The correct answer is C

A. Customer demand is a strategic consideration because it is a forecast of what the customer will want in the future and the companies strategic goals should include the desire to fulfill this demand.
B. The chance to achieve a strategic opportunity is a clear strategic consideration for authorizing a project
C. Return on investment is not a strategic consideration. It is a method of calculating whether a project should proceed from a financial rather than strategic point of view.
D. Market demand is a strategic consideration because it is a forecast of what how the market will be behaving in the future and the companies strategic goals should include the desire to fulfill this demand.

11: The correct answer is D

A. A war room is a specific meeting room for project team members to be collocated and focus on doing the project work.
B. Although sometimes the acronym PMO does stand for Program Management Office, it is more commonly used to refer to a Project Management Office which is the correct answer.
C. Project headquarters is not correct although the term may be used by some organizations it is not part of the standardized terminology offered by the PMBOK® Guide.
D. A project management office (PMO) takes responsibility for providing organization-wide project management support functions, including common standards, templates and processes. It is also directly responsible for project delivery.

12: The correct answer is B

A. A clear role of a mature PMO would be to oversee and manage shared resources across several projects.
B. A PMO provides high level support across several projects. It does not provide lower level detail to a single project but would instead provide a rolled up summary report of the project.

C. A role of a PMO is to development and improve an organizations project management methodology.
D. One very clear role of any sort of PMO is to ensure communications across projects is done effectively.

13: The correct answer is B

A. A project life cycle and the product life cycle certainly do intersect during the development of a new product as it is a project.
B. Notice that this question uses the PRODUCT life cycle, not the PROJECT life cycle. You will need to look out for this style of question and make sure you read it properly. The product lifecycle covers all aspects of the product from inception, design and manufacture to end of life, recycling and obsolescence. Monitoring and controlling are one of the five process groups.
C. Improvements in operations can be delivered by defining them as a project and as such projects do intersect with operational activities at this point.
D. During closeout phases the deliverable is handed over to operations and as such there is a clear intersection between the project and operational activities.

14: The correct answer is D

A. Organizational strategy will not operate at a level that influences the appointment of the project manager.
B. Organizational strategy does not directly link to project governance.
C. Organizational strategy and project management do interact as project management as seen as a strategic enabler for organizations.
D. Successful projects enable organizations to deliver their strategic goals.

15: The correct answer is D

A. Business value is based on actual tangible and intangible value. Projects that are underway would form a small part of this overall value.
B. In addition to the value created by projects, business value also includes intangible elements as well.
C. Business value is defined as the sum of both tangible and intangible elements

D. Business value is defined as the sum of all tangible and intangible elements including things such as monetary assets, fixtures, equity, goodwill, brand recognition and trademarks.

16: The correct answer is D

A. A program manager is responsible for sharing resources among projects.
B. A project team member would be responsible for delivery of the technical tasks.
C. While a project manager does have responsibility for controlling the budget in most instances this is not the best description offered from the available answers.
D. The project manager is the person vested with the authority by the performing organization to achieve the objectives of the project.

17: The correct answer is C

A. Government standards and industry regulations are a great example of enterprise environmental factors as they can effect a project.
B. The political climate that a project operates in is an enterprise environmental factor.
C. Net present value of investment is a tool for project selection.
D. Project management information systems as an example of organizational process assets not enterprise environmental factors.

18: The correct answer is D

A. The interdependency of projects within a program of work is an example of an organizations program management not OPM3.
B. An assessment of the level of variance between project management best practice and the actual application of these practices would be part of an assessment of project management maturity but is not the best description of OPM3.
C. The ability of a project manager to successfully deliver a project is an example of a individual project managers level of professional development and not OPM3.

D. OPM3 stands for Organizational Project Management Maturity Model and part of the model is used to assess where on a scale an organization sits in relation to its adoption and application of project management practices.

19: The correct answer is B

A. This answer is not correct because it is not a term referenced within the PMBOK® Guide.

B. Enterprise environmental factors are a pretty constant input into many of the processes. They can be thought of as the environment in which the project must operate and by which it will be influenced.

C. This answer is not correct because it is not a term referenced within the PMBOK® Guide.

D. This answer is not correct because it is not a term referenced within the PMBOK® Guide.

20: The correct answer is B

A. A project management methodology is a prescribed and standardized approach to project management and does not describe overlapping project phases.

B. Knowing the project life cycle and how projects and project management fit gives you context and provides a basic framework for managing a project, regardless of the specific work involved. Do not get this confused with PRODUCT life cycle.

C. A Project Management Office (PMO) is the center of excellence for project management within an organization and does not refer to a collection of overlapping phases.

D. The project management information system is an example of an organizational process asset and does not refer to a collection of overlapping phases.

21: The correct answer is A

A. The generic level of the project life cycle features four key characteristics of starting the project, organizing and preparing, carrying out the project work, and closing the project. Checking the project is part of the Shewhart and Deming Plan-Do-Check-

B. Closing the project is the final step in the project life cycle.

C. Starting the project is the first step in the project life cycle.
D. Carrying out the project work is a characteristic of the project life cycle.

22: The correct answer is B

A. There are costs associated with his part of the project life cycle but they are not as high as carrying out the project work which has the greatest assignment resources and activities.
B. Generally speaking, cost and staffing levels are highest during the phase in the project life cycle where work is being carried out.
C. There are costs associated with his part of the project life cycle but they are not as high as carrying out the project work which has the greatest assignment resources and activities.
D. There are costs associated with his part of the project life cycle but they are not as high as carrying out the project work which has the greatest assignment resources and activities.

23: The correct answer is C

A. Stakeholders are able to influence the project during project execution but not as much as they can at the beginning of the project/
B. Toward the end of the project stakeholders have less influence as the deliverable is close to completion
C. The higher levels of uncertainty at the beginning of project, reflecting the process of progressive elaboration, mean that stakeholders can have more influence during this time at the beginning of a project.
D. Stakeholder influence is greatest at the beginning of a project and slowly diminishes as the project progresses.

24: The correct answer is D

A. The cost of changes increases the more your proceed through a project as greater commitment is made to the deliverable and the resources to produce the deliverable.
B. The cost of changes is lowest at the beginning of the project as very little commitment has been made at this point to resources and executing the work.
C. There will be significant cost of changes during project execution but they wont be as much as towards the end of the project.

D. As you near the end of the project both the cost and impact of any requested changes increase.

25: The correct answer is D

A. Sub-projects is an informal term used to describe smaller subsets of work but it does not refer to divisions in the project.
B. Stage gate may be a common term but it is not the term used in the standardized terminology offered by the PMBOK® Guide.
C. Decision trees are ways of assessing quantifiable risk and do not refer to divisions within a project.
D. You may decide to initiate phases in a project due to the size, complexity or presence of defined major deliverables. Breaking such projects down into phases gives a greater level of control.

26: The correct answer is B

A. Generally phases are performed sequentially as a deliverable from one phase provides input into the next. However, depending on the type of project and the interaction between phase deliverables there can also be overlapping and iterative relationships be
B. The three types of phase-to-phase relationships are overlapping, iterative and sequential. Progressive is not one of these.
C. Generally phases are performed sequentially as a deliverable from one phase provides input into the next. However, depending on the type of project and the interaction between phase deliverables there can also be overlapping and iterative relationships be
D. The three types of phase-to-phase relationships are overlapping, iterative and sequential.

27: The correct answer is C

A. A team member is a specific type of stakeholder. Stakeholder is the best answer to this questions.
B. A customer is a specific type of stakeholder. Stakeholder is the best answer to this questions.
C. A stakeholder is anyone or any organization who can affect or be affected by the project. It is important to identify all stakeholders on a project and manage or influence their expectations.

D. A sponsor is a specific type of stakeholder. Stakeholder is the best answer to this questions.

28: The correct answer is A

A. This situation describes a matrix organization where the functional manager retains most of the power. Therefore, it is a weak matrix, reflecting the small amount of power the project manager has to influence resources and budget on the project.
B. In a strong matrix the project manager, not the functional manager, would have most power.
C. The questions refers to some staff working for you implying there are other staff from other functional areas working for you and as such it indicates a matrix form of organization, specifically a weak matrix.
D. In a projectized structure the project manager would have full responsibility and authority.

29: The correct answer is A

A. This situation describes an organization divided into its functional responsibilities. A project manager will often have to deal with staff and resources from different areas across the organization that are ultimately controlled by the functional manager
B. Any sort of matrix organization has staff working across different functional areas and as such this questions outlines a functional organizational structure.
C. Any sort of matrix organization has staff working across different functional areas and as such this questions outlines a functional organizational structure.
D. In a projectized structure the project manager would have full responsibility and authority.

30: The correct answer is C

A. Any sort of templates are an example of organizational process assets as they are owned by the organization and can be used to assist projects.
B. Lessons learned are an example of organizational process assets as they are owned by the organization and can be used to assist projects.

C. Government regulations are an example of Enterprise Environmental Factors. The other three are examples of Organizational Process Assets which belong to the company, are the property of the company, and reflect the organizational culture.

D. Configuration management knowledge bases are an example of organizational process assets as they are owned by the organization and can be used to assist projects.

31: The correct answer is D

A. Standardization is not correct because every project is different.

B. Taking a prudent view when deciding which processes, tools and techniques are appropriate would be correct but tailoring is the term used to describe the process of doing this.

C. Customizing may generally describe the process of tailoring but it is not the terminology offered in the PMBOK® Guide.

D. The processes described in the PMBOK® Guide are not to be universally applied to every project. Each project is different. It is the responsibility of the project manager and project team to determine which processes are appropriate and how rigorously the

32: The correct answer is B

A. The executing process carries out the work planned.

B. The initiating process group is always the first performed in any project or phase of a project. It is the process group that formally establishes the project.

C. The closing process closes the project

D. The planning process builds on the work done during the initiating process.

33: The correct answer is D

A. The monitoring and controlling process checks that the work being done matches what was planned and manages any requested changes.

B. The planning process builds on the work done during the initiating process.

C. The initiating process group is always the first performed in any project or phase of a project. It is the process group that formally establishes the project.

D. The executing process group consists of those processes that complete the work defined in the project management plan.

34: The correct answer is A

A. Project Integration Management has 6 processes in it. They are Develop Project Charter, Develop Project Management Plan, Direct and Manage Project Work, Monitor and Control Project Work, Perform Integrated Change Control, and Close Project or Phase.
B. Project Integration Management has 6 processes in it. They are Develop Project Charter, Develop Project Management Plan, Direct and Manage Project Work, Monitor and Control Project Work, Perform Integrated Change Control, and Close Project or Phase.
C. Project Integration Management has 6 processes in it. They are Develop Project Charter, Develop Project Management Plan, Direct and Manage Project Work, Monitor and Control Project Work, Perform Integrated Change Control, and Close Project or Phase.
D. Project Integration Management has 6 processes in it. They are Develop Project Charter, Develop Project Management Plan, Direct and Manage Project Work, Monitor and Control Project Work, Perform Integrated Change Control, and Close Project or Phase.

35: The correct answer is B

A. Develop Project Management Plan is a specific process not a knowledge area.
B. Project Integration Management is the process of understanding the interaction and interdependencies between all the different knowledge areas.
C. Project Risk Management is a specific process not a knowledge area.
D. Perform Integrated Change Control is a specific process not a knowledge area.

36: The correct answer is D

A. The PMBOK® Guide is a framework from which you select the appropriate knowledge, skills and processes to apply a professional and rigorous project management approach appropriate to the size, industry and complexity of your particular project.

B. The PMBOK® Guide is a framework from which you select the appropriate knowledge, skills and processes to apply a professional and rigorous project management approach appropriate to the size, industry and complexity of your particular project.

C. The PMBOK® Guide is a framework from which you select the appropriate knowledge, skills and processes to apply a professional and rigorous project management approach appropriate to the size, industry and complexity of your particular project.

D. The PMBOK® Guide is a framework from which you select the appropriate knowledge, skills and processes to apply a professional and rigorous project management approach appropriate to the size, industry and complexity of your particular project.

37: The correct answer is D

A. The project charter should be the document that appoints the project manager.

B. The project charter should always contain information about the project initiation.

C. The project charter should contain a high level description of the work to be done on the project.

D. The project charter is like the birth certificate for a project. You need it to prove the project exists and to provide basic but extremely important information about the project. The information it contains is generally quite high level; it is the first

38: The correct answer is D

A. The project authorization memo is not a term referenced within the PMBOK® Guide.

B. There are several issues outlined in this question but the root cause could be determined by examining a foundational document such as the project charter.

C. The cost performance analysis and report wont help deal with any underlying issues as it will merely report status.

D. The project charter is the document that formally authorizes a project. The project charter is the document issued by the sponsor that formally authorizes the project and provides the project manager with the authority to apply organizational resources to

39: The correct answer is C

A. Enterprise environmental factors like market conditions and industry regulations would definitely be considered as part of the development of the project charter.
B. The business case can definitely be used as an input into the project charter as it contains information about the financial justification for the project.
C. At the stage of developing the project charter you do not have a project management plan so it can't be an input
D. The project statement work is a high level narrative description of the work to be done on the project and as such would be part of the development of the project charter.

40: The correct answer is B

A. There is no need for the project charter to have a copy of the stakeholder register and the project charter is an input into the Identify Stakeholders process which process the stakeholder register.
B. The business case contains information to enable the project sponsor to authorize the project from a business perspective and as such must contain information about expected market demand for the product
C. Blank templates will be part of the development of the project charter but not necessarily part of the business case.
D. The project management plan is done after the development of the project charter and as such would not be included in the business case.

41: The correct answer is D

A. Product scope description is not a term referenced within the PMBOK® Guide.
B. The project scope statement is a detailed, not high level, description of the work to be done.
C. The project scope is another name for the project scope statement which is a detailed, not high level, description of the work to be done.
D. The project statement of work is a high level document used as an input in the development of the project charter.

42: The correct answer is C

A. You would expect to see NPV used to justify a project on financial grounds.
B. You would expect to see ROI used to justify a project on financial grounds.
C. External rate of investment (ERI) is not a term referenced within the PMBOK® Guide.
D. You would expect to see IRR used to justify a project on financial grounds.

43: The correct answer is C

A. The statement of work will include a high level description of the project scope.
B. The statement of work will include a description of the business need for the project.
C. The staffing plan is not part of the statement of work (SOW). Did you get confused by all the information in this question? You must be able to dissect a question and understand exactly what is it asking. In this instance the question is in the last sente
D. The statement of work will refer to the strategic plan and how the project delivers strategic goals.

44: The correct answer is D

A. Although a business case may be part of the project charter, business case preparation is not one of the listed tools or techniques if the Develop Charter process.
B. The Delphi technique is a specific type of information gathering technique and it is not used in the Develop Project Charter process
C. Analytical techniques are a tool or technique used in the Close Project or Phase, and Monitor and Control Project Work processes.
D. Expert judgment is used to assess the inputs used in the development of the project charter.

45: The correct answer is D

A. The quality management plan relates to project quality and will not be detailed enough to give you all the information you require.
B. The project statement of work will not be detailed enough to give you all the information you require.

C. The project charter will not be detailed enough to give you all the information you require.

D. The project management plan is a product of all the different knowledge areas and contains the information required to execute, monitor and control, and close the project.

46: The correct answer is D

A. The communications management plan is an output from another process, specifically the Plan Communications Management process, and as such it is an input into the Develop Project Management Plan process.

B. The project charter provides the authorization to begin the planning processes which deliver the project management plan.

C. The process improvement plan is an output from another process, specifically the Plan Quality Management process, and as such it is an input into the Develop Project Management Plan process.

D. Work performance information is not a direct input into the development of the project management plan.

47: The correct answer is D

A. The application of professional project management practices does not guarantee project success, but it does increase the chances of project success. Projects seldom run exactly according to the project management plan, which is why we have the integrated change control process. The project management plan and the project scope statement must be maintained by carefully and continuously managing changes.

B. Using the Crticial Chain Method will not completley eliminate any possible changes. Projects seldom run exactly according to the project management plan, which is why we have the integrated change control process. The project management plan and the project scope statement must be maintained by carefully and continuously managing changes.

C. Unfortunately good planning does not give precise knowledge about how a project will perform, it gives an idea of how you plan for it to perform. Projects seldom run exactly according to the project management plan, which is why we have the integrated change control process. The project management plan and the project scope statement must be maintained by carefully and continuously managing changes.

D. Projects seldom run exactly according to the project management plan, which is why we have the integrated change control process. The project management plan and the project scope statement must be maintained by carefully and continuously managing changes

48: The correct answer is C

A. The project management plan contains the project scope and how the work will be executed to achieve this scope.
B. The project management plan can be either summary or detailed depending on the timing and complexity of the project and what is required to successfully plan it.
C. This description outlines the contents of a project charter not the project management plan.
D. The project management plan is a collection of all the other planning documents and subsidiary plans from the other planning processes.

49: The correct answer is A

A. While it may be your experience that a project management plan is rarely used, the best answer is that this document will vary depending upon the application area and complexity of the project.
B. It is the last part of this answer which makes in incorrect. Project management plans are not similar regardless of the complexity of the project.
C. It is the last part of this answer which makes in incorrect. Project management plans are always used in practice.
D. It is the last part of this answer which makes in incorrect. Project management plans are not an input into the project charter process.

50: The correct answer is C

A. Product scope analysis is not a term referenced within the PMBOK® Guide.
B. Project management information systems are not used during the Develop Project Management Plan process.
C. Expert judgment is used to assess the inputs used in the development of the project management plan.

D. Business case preparation is done as part of the Develop Project Charter process and is not used during the Develop Project Management Plan process.

51: The correct answer is C

A. There is no communication baseline.
B. There is no risk management baseline.
C. The performance measurement baseline is a combination of the scope, schedule, and cost baselines. Remember that you use the performance measurement baseline for your earned value measurements.
D. There is no procurement baseline.

52: The correct answer is A

A. Lessons learned are not part of the change control process itself. Although you may use the change requests you received in an analysis of what went well and not so well on the project.
B. The Direct and Manage Project Work process requires implementation of preventative actions
C. The Direct and Manage Project Work process requires implementation of corrective actions
D. The Direct and Manage Project Work process requires implementation of any identified defects needing repair.

53: The correct answer is A

A. Development of the project charter is not part of the execution of the project management plan. It is part of project initiation.
B. Managing identified risks is part of the work to be done as each risk response strategy represents project work.
C. Team members are essential for getting the planed work completed.
D. Monitoring and controlling the work being done against what was planned is an essential part of the execution phase.

54: The correct answer is B

A. The project management plan is used as a key input into the Direct and Manage Project Work process as it outlines all the work to be done.

B. Work performance data is an output of the Direct and Manage Project Work process.

C. Approved change requests are an input as they represent work to be done on the project.

D. Enterprise environmental factors such as market conditions and legislation are an important consideration and input in to the Direct and Manage Project Work process.

55: The correct answer is C

A. Issue and defect management procedures is an example of an organizational process asset.

B. The process measurement database is an example of an organizational process asset.

C. This is a tough question that tests your knowledge of the difference between organizational process assets and enterprise environmental factors. Stakeholder risk tolerances are an enterprise environmental factor as they are part of the environment in whic

D. Standardized guidelines and work instructions are an example of organizational process assets.

56: The correct answer is A

A. Work performance data provides information on the status of the project activities being performed to accomplish the project work.

B. Project management plan updates would not provide information about the schedule or quality standards.

C. The project deliverables would not provide information about the schedule or quality standards.

D. Change requests would not provide information about the schedule or quality standards.

57: The correct answer is A

A. The question is the PMBOK® Guide definition of the Monitor and Control Project Work process.

B. The Direct and Manage Project Work process executes the project management plan.

C. The Perform Integrated Change Control process monitors, assesses and controls change requests.

D. *The Develop Project Management Plan process produces the project management plan.*

58: The correct answer is D

A. *Expert judgment, analytical techniques, project management information systems and meetings are the tools and techniques used in the Monitor and Control Project Work*
B. *Expert judgment, analytical techniques, project management information systems and meetings are the tools and techniques used in the Monitor and Control Project Work*
C. *Expert judgment, analytical techniques, project management information systems and meetings are the tools and techniques used in the Monitor and Control Project Work*
D. *The Delphi technique is not a tool used in the Monitor and Control Project Work process. It is a powerful information gathering technique that can be used in many situations where you want expert opinion but want to build consensus as well. Key elements are that it is iterative and anonymous which eliminates peer pressure.*

59: The correct answer is D

A. *Change requests, work performance reports, project management plan updates and project documents updates are the four outputs from the Monitor and Control Project work process.*
B. *Change requests, work performance reports, project management plan updates and project documents updates are the four outputs from the Monitor and Control Project work process.*
C. *Change requests, work performance reports, project management plan updates and project documents updates are the four outputs from the Monitor and Control Project work process.*
D. *Work performance information is input to, not an output from, the Monitor and Control Project Work process. During the process it becomes work performance reports.*

60: The correct answer is B

A. *You would perform integrated change control during the project execution phase as well as performing it from inception to completion so this answer is not correct.*

B. Changes can affect a project at any point in the lifecycle and therefore you must be ready to proactively influence, monitor and control change requests.

C. You would perform integrated change control during the monitoring and controlling phase as well as performing it from inception to completion so this answer is not correct.

D. This answer is not correct because it does not acknowledge that integrated change control is also performed during project initiation and project planning phases.

61: The correct answer is B

A. This answer is correct because all change requests must have a decision made about them

B. The word ALL in this answer makes it incorrect as the project manager can have a level of delegated authority to approve or decline requested changes so they don't all need to go to the change control board.

C. A change request may be initiated verbally but should always be recorded in a document of some sort.

D. A change request in one area, quality for example, may have impacts in other areas such as cost, time and risk.

62: The correct answer is B

A. A risk management system is not focused on consistently validating and improving the project by recording and considering the impact of each change. It is focused on identification, assessment and responses to risk.

B. Project-wide application of the configuration management system, including change control processes, accomplishes three main objectives:1. Establishes an evaluation method to consistently identify and request changes to established baselines; 2. Provides opportunities to continuously validate and improve the project by considering the impact of each change; 3. Provides the mechanism for the project management team to consistently communicate all changes to stakeholders.

C. A project management information systems (PMIS)is not focused on consistently validating and improving the project by recording and considering the impact of each change. It is focused on storage and retrieval of project management information..

D. A work authorization system is not focused on consistently validating and improving the project by recording and considering the impact of each change.

63: The correct answer is C

A. This answer is correct because it does describe an important objective of the configuration management system.
B. This answer is correct because it does describe an important objective of the configuration management system.
C. This answer is incorrect because it describes part of the change control process not the configuration management system.
D. This answer is correct because it does describe an important objective of the configuration management system.

64: The correct answer is B

A. This answer is correct because it does describe an important attribute of the configuration management system.
B. This answer is incorrect because the configuration management system controls and records changes; it does not prevent them.
C. This answer is correct because it does describe an important attribute of the configuration management system.
D. This answer is correct because it does describe an important attribute of the configuration management system.

65: The correct answer is B

A. Configuration identification is one the core activities of configuration management, included in the integrated change control process.
B. Configuration control and assessment may sound like a correct answer but it is not a term referenced within the PMBOK® Guide.
C. Configuration status accounting is one the core activities of configuration management, included in the integrated change control process.
D. Configuration verification and audit is one the core activities of configuration management, included in the integrated change control process.

66: The correct answer is D

A. The Develop Project Management Plan process produces the project management plan and does not process change requests.
B. The Direct and Manage Project Work process executes the planned work and does not process change requests.
C. The Monitor and Control Project Work process identifies any variances from planned baselines and raises change requests but does not process change requests.
D. Project changes can require new or revised cost estimates, schedule dates, resource requirements and other project deliverables. These changes can require adjustments to the project management plan project scope statement, or other project deliverables. Y

67: The correct answer is D

A. The inputs into the Perform Integrated Change Control process are the project management plan, work performance reports, change requests, enterprise environmental factors, and organizational process assets.
B. The inputs into the Perform Integrated Change Control process are the project management plan, work performance reports, change requests, enterprise environmental factors, and organizational process assets.
C. The inputs into the Perform Integrated Change Control process are the project management plan, work performance reports, change requests, enterprise environmental factors, and organizational process assets.
D. Project document updates are an output of, not an input to, the Perform Integrated Change Control process.

68: The correct answer is D

A. This answer is wrong because it is silly to think that there is conflict of interest simply because someone raises a change request.
B. If the change request is feasible it should definitely be considered and not just declined
C. The project sponsor was either consulted or informed about the change as part of the normal integrated change control process so there is no special reason to inform them now.
D. Making changes to a project that are not part of the project scope is acceptable as long as the relevant process is followed and the relevant baseline is changed to reflect the new information. Remember that a baseline is the original baseline plus any approved changes.

69: The correct answer is A

A. The process of closing and finalizing any contracts is done during the Close Procurements process.
B. This answer is correct because it describes an important characteristic of the Close Project or Phase process.
C. This answer is correct because it describes an important characteristic of the Close Project or Phase process.
D. This answer is correct because it describes an important characteristic of the Close Project or Phase process.

70: The correct answer is C

A. The project management plan, accepted deliverables and organizational process assets are all inputs in the Close Project or Phase process.
B. The project management plan, accepted deliverables and organizational process assets are all inputs in the Close Project or Phase process.
C. Work performance information is an input into several other processes but not the Close Project or Phase process.
D. The project management plan, accepted deliverables and organizational process assets are all inputs in the Close Project or Phase process.

71: The correct answer is C

A. This answer is incorrect because it is entirely unprofessional to shred documents which could be used later when the project restarts.
B. You cannot ignore a request like this as there is no funding to continue the project.
C. If a project is terminated prior to completion, the formal documentation indicates why the project was terminated, and formalizes the procedures for the transfer of the finished and unfinished deliverables of the project to others.
D. The question clearly outlines that there is no budget for your project so you must assume that this has already been done by those people responsible for funding projects.

72: The correct answer is D

A. *Project files, project closure documents and historical information are all examples of organizational process assets that would be updated.*
B. *Project files, project closure documents and historical information are all examples of organizational process assets that would be updated.*
C. *Project files, project closure documents and historical information are all examples of organizational process assets that would be updated.*
D. *The stakeholder risk tolerance register would not be considered an organizational process asset.*

73: The correct answer is C

A. *In this instance you are being asked to add functionality that is not in the scope. To do so without going through a formal change control process which would involve the customer would be an example of gold plating. Remember that at all times you must always be delivering only what is documented. There is no problem delivering more but it must be thoroughly documented and approved.*
B. *In this instance you are being asked to add functionality that is not in the scope. To do so without going through a formal change control process which would involve the customer would be an example of gold plating. Remember that at all times you must always be delivering only what is documented. There is no problem delivering more but it must be thoroughly documented and approved.*
C. *In this instance you are being asked to add functionality that is not in the scope. To do so without going through a formal change control process which would involve the customer would be an example of gold plating. Remember that at all times you must always be delivering only what is documented. There is no problem delivering more but it must be thoroughly documented and approved.*
D. *In this instance you are being asked to add functionality that is not in the scope. To do so without going through a formal change control process which would involve the customer would be an example of gold plating. Remember that at all times you must always be delivering only what is documented. There is no problem delivering more but it must be thoroughly documented and approved.*

74: The correct answer is A

A. You will probably not have to calculate NPV in the exam that you may be resented with a similar question. In this case it is possible to use a rule of thumb to simply add up the total revenue generated and subtract from that the cost of the project and then discount this by 10% over four years. Using this rule of thumb you can see that none of the other answers could be correct and that this answer is probably the correct one. If you did use the NPV formula to calculate the answer you would have calculated that within a few dollars of $41,000.

B. $100,000 represents the spend on the project in the first year, not the NPV. You will probably not have to calculate NPV in the exam that you may be resented with a similar question. In this case it is possible to use a rule of thumb to simply add up the total revenue generated and subtract from that the cost of the project and then discount this by 10% over four years. Using this rule of thumb you can see that none of the other answers could be correct and that this answer is probably the correct one. If you did use the NPV formula to calculate the answer you would have calculated that with a few dollars $41,000.

C. $ $80,000 represents the total revenue generated from the project with the cost of a project subtracted not the NPV. You will probably not have to calculate NPV in the exam that you may be resented with a similar question. In this case it is possible to use a rule of thumb to simply add up the total revenue generated and subtract from that the cost of the project and then discount this by 10% over four years. Using this rule of thumb you can see that none of the other answers could be correct and that this answer is probably the correct one. If you did use the NPV formula to calculate that within a few dollars of $41,000.

D. You would have arrived at $280,000. If you simply added the four figures in the question together, and they do not represent the NPV.

75: The correct answer is A

A. Between the two projects Project Eagle has the higher NPV and as such it should be preferred option.

B. The cost of Project Falcon has already been taken into account with the NPV calculation and therefore you should choose the project with a higher NPV which is project Eagle.

C. The question present enough information to enable you to compare NPV between the two projects and you should choose a project with a higher NPV.

D. In order for a project ahead it must have a positive NPV and both projects do. You should choose a project with the highest NPV.

76: The correct answer is A

A. The question gives you lots of information about net present value and the cost of each project but the only relevant information is the net present value because it is recalculated the cost.
B. The question gives you lots of information about net present value and the cost of each project but the only relevant information is the net present value because it is recalculated the cost. Therefore, you should choose a project with the highest net present value which is project B.
C. The question gives you lots of information about net present value and the cost of each project but the only relevant information is the net present value because it is recalculated the cost.
D. The question gives you lots of information about net present value and the cost of each project but the only relevant information is the net present value because it is recalculated the cost.

77: The correct answer is C

A. When faced with a choice between two projects the opportunity cost is the benefit that would be derived by doing the other project. Therefore in this case opportunity cost of performing project B is the benefit of project A which is $75,000.
B. When faced with a choice between two projects the opportunity cost is the benefit that would be derived by doing the other project. Therefore in this case opportunity cost of performing project B is the benefit of project A which is $75,000.
C. When faced with a choice between two projects the opportunity cost is the benefit that would be derived by doing the other project. Therefore in this case opportunity cost of performing project B is the benefit of project A which is $75,000.
D. When faced with a choice between two projects the opportunity cost is the benefit that would be derived by doing the other project. Therefore in this case opportunity cost of performing project B is the benefit of project A which is $75,000.

78: The correct answer is A

A. Project scope management makes it clear that at times you should ensure you are delivering only what is documented. This allows for change to occur but makes it clear that you should document all changes to the baseline and ensure you are delivering exactly what has been documented.
B. Project baseline delivery is incorrect because it is not a term referenced within the PMBOK® Guide.
C. Project specification delivery is incorrect because it is not a term referenced within the PMBOK® Guide.
D. Project management execution is incorrect because it is not a term referenced within the PMBOK® Guide.

79: The correct answer is D

A. If you are able to assess the request and approve it via your approved change control process there is no reason to simply decline it. You should always look for ways to deliver more that what was expected as long as it is documented.
B. If you are able to assess the request and approve it via your approved change control process there is no reason to simply decline it. You should always look for ways to deliver more that what was expected as long as it is documented.
C. The first step before doing this option is to assess the change via your change control process.
D. This is an issue about 'gold plating' which in effect means you are delivering more than what you were required to do. While this sounds like a good thing to do, it also means you are not delivering what has been documented. There are no problems with seizing the opportunity to deliver more but you must always be delivering what is agreed and documented. So in this case you would formally assess the change; if it gets accepted by your change control process you would then amend the necessary documents so that at all times you are delivering exactly what is documented.

80: The correct answer is D

A. The scope baseline is made up of the detailed project scope statement (which will include all approved changes), the WBS and the WBS dictionary which provides all the additional information needed to fully understand the WBS.

B. The scope baseline is made up of the detailed project scope statement (which will include all approved changes), the WBS and the WBS dictionary which provides all the additional information needed to fully understand the WBS.

C. The scope baseline is made up of the detailed project scope statement (which will include all approved changes), the WBS and the WBS dictionary which provides all the additional information needed to fully understand the WBS.

D. The scope baseline is made up of the detailed project scope statement (which will include all approved changes), the WBS and the WBS dictionary which provides all the additional information needed to fully understand the WBS.

81: The correct answer is B

A. First you must always have the project charter; with it, you can determine the requirements documentation. Both of these are then inputs into the Define Scope process, which produces the project scope statement.
B. First you must always have the project charter; with it, you can determine the requirements documentation. Both of these are then inputs into the Define Scope process, which produces the project scope statement.
C. First you must always have the project charter; with it, you can determine the requirements documentation.
D. First you must always have the project charter; with it, you can determine the requirements documentation.

82: The correct answer is C

A. The requirements traceability matrix is an output from the Collect Requirements process and links product requirements from their origin to the deliverables that satisfy them.
B. The scope management plan is focused upon the definition, documentation and management of the entire project scope
C. The requirements management plan is a part of the project management plan that describes how requirements will be analyzed, documented and managed?
D. This answer is not correct because it is not a term referenced within the PMBOK® Guide.

83: The correct answer is A

A. The product scope is measured against the documented product requirements gathered during the Collect Requirements process.
B. The scope management plan is focused upon the definition, documentation and management of the entire project scope
C. The project management plan contains the project scope and how the work will be executed to achieve this scope, not just the product scope.
D. Client expectations are captured in the requirements documentation of which a subset will be the product requirements.

84: The correct answer is B

A. This is an important distinction that you learn and look out for in the exam. Watch out for the use of PROJECT and PRODUCT when reading the questions as each is different. Project requirements relate to the way the project is delivered while product requirements relate to the technical requirements of the product.
B. This is an important distinction that you learn and look out for in the exam. Watch out for the use of PROJECT and PRODUCT when reading the questions as each is different. Project requirements relate to the way the project is delivered while product requirements relate to the technical requirements of the product.
C. This is an important distinction that you learn and look out for in the exam. Watch out for the use of PROJECT and PRODUCT when reading the questions as each is different. Project requirements relate to the way the project is delivered while product requirements relate to the technical requirements of the product.
D. This is an important distinction that you learn and look out for in the exam. Watch out for the use of PROJECT and PRODUCT when reading the questions as each is different. Project requirements relate to the way the project is delivered while product requirements relate to the technical requirements of the product.

85: The correct answer is A

A. Collect Requirements defines and documents stakeholders needs by producing the requirements documentation, requirements management plan and the requirements traceability matrix.
B. Project integration management is a knowledge area not a process.
C. Project scope management is a knowledge area not a process.

D. *This answer is incorrect because it is not a PMBOK® Guide process.*

86: The correct answer is D

A. This answer is not correct because questioning should be encouraged amongst team members.
B. The project management plan is not the best place to look for the original requirements and product description. The project charter is the best place to look for original descriptions.
C. The project scope statement is not the best place to look for the original requirements and product description. The project charter is the best place to look for original descriptions.
D. The project charter is the founding document for the project. At the time it is developed, agreed and approved, generally only high level information about the project requirements and product description is known but at all times the project should be al

87: The correct answer is B

A. There are number of techniques for soliciting information about requirements from the relevant stakeholders. Focus groups are one of these techniques.
B. A requirements traceability matrix is an output of the Collect Requirements process.
C. There are number of techniques for soliciting information about requirements from the relevant stakeholders. Group decision making techniques are one of these techniques.
D. There are number of techniques for soliciting information about requirements from the relevant stakeholders. Interviews are one of these techniques.

88: The correct answer is A

A. The Delphi technique is a powerful information gathering technique that can be used in many situations where you want expert opinion but want to build consensus as well. Key elements are that it is iterative and anonymous which eliminates peer pressure an
B. The nominal group technique is the incorrect answer because it is a way to get a decisions from a group by considering all possible decisions and getting group members to rank their support for each one.

C. Brainstorming is incorrect because it is a method of getting a group to think laterally, or outside the square, and consider a wide range of ideas.
D. Mind mapping is incorrect because it is a graphical technique use to link ideas together.

89: The correct answer is D

A. Scope definition is not a PMBOK® Guide process.
B. The Develop Project Charter process provides the project charter not the requirements documentation.
C. The Project Scope Management knowledge area contains all the processes for planning, defining and checking the project scope and the requirements documentation is a small subset of this.
D. Collect Requirements produces your requirements documentation, requirements management plan and the requirements traceability matrix.

90: The correct answer is D

A. The business need, acceptance criteria and Business rules stating the guiding principles of the organization are all important components of the requirements documentation.
B. The business need, acceptance criteria and Business rules stating the guiding principles of the organization are all important components of the requirements documentation.
C. The business need, acceptance criteria and Business rules stating the guiding principles of the organization are all important components of the requirements documentation.
D. The requirements documentation describes how individual requirements meet the business need for the project. Configuration management activities are a component of the requirements management plan not the requirements documentation.

91: The correct answer is B

A. The Collect Requirements process identifies and documents the project and product requirements from stakeholders and does not relate to using the requirements documentation to begin the process of developing a detailed description of the project and produ

B. Define Scope is the process of developing your detailed description of both the project and product. Having a detailed scope statement is critical to project success. Remember that this process will be iterative and can be fully developed as the project moves along.
C. The Plan Scope Management process seeks to define the process for describing and controlling the projects scope.
D. The Define Activities process is part of the Project Time Management knowledge area and does not relate to using the requirements documentation to begin the process of developing a detailed description of the project and product.

92: The correct answer is A

A. Stakeholder analysis is correct because it is likely that some of the stakeholders' requirements were not incorporated into the scope definition of the project, resulting in deliverables missing from the WBS and the project schedule.
B. Critical path analysis is not part of the Scope Management knowledge area. Critical path analysis is competed after the project schedule is done and is part of Time Management.
C. The integrated change control project receives, assess and approves or declines change requests and is not part of the Scope Management processes. Integrated change control is done during the monitoring and controlling of a project.
D. Although decomposition is an important step in Scope Management and is necessary to generate the WBS, it is the subdivision of project deliverables into smaller, more manageable work components

93: The correct answer is D

A. The inputs into the Define Scope process are the scope management plan, project charter, requirements documentation and organizational process assets.
B. The inputs into the Define Scope process are the scope management plan, project charter, requirements documentation and organizational process assets.
C. The inputs into the Define Scope process are the scope management plan, project charter, requirements documentation and organizational process assets.

D. The project scope statement is an output from, not an input into, the Define Scope process.

94: The correct answer is A

A. During subsequent phases of multi-phase projects, the project scope statement defines and validates (if necessary) the project scope.
B. The project management plan contains all the subsidiary plans for executing the project. But the project scope statement is the best answer for this question.
C. The statement of work would not contain enough information to be useful in this situation.
D. The requirements traceability matrix links the original requirements to the deliverables that are supposed to met them and would not be of assistance in this situation.

95: The correct answer is B

A. You may use the term tasks but it is not a standard term used in the PMBOK® Guide.
B. When you undertake the process of decomposition to complete your WBS, you break down the deliverables into smaller, more manageable components. The smallest level in the WBS is the work package. A work package can be further divided into activities but this is beyond the WBS.
C. Activities are work packages that are decomposed eve further but they are too detailed to be included as part of the WBS.
D. Units is not a term referenced within the PMBOK® Guide.

96: The correct answer is A

A. Developing a robust WBS is critical to the success of your project as it defines all the work packages that must be completed. The process of doing this is the Create WBS process.
B. Define activities breaks down work packages even further than work packages and is not part of the Create WBS process which is the best answer.
C. The Define Scope process does just what it sounds like and defines the project and product scope but does not break it down.

D. The Collect Requirements process gathers stakeholder requirements for inclusion in the project scope but it does not subdivide project deliverables and project work into smaller components

97: The correct answer is D

A. Decomposition of the Scope using the WBS does mean the planned work within the lowest levels can be scheduled, cost estimated, monitored, and controlled
B. The WBS is a deliverable-oriented hierarchical decomposition of the work to be executed by the project team.
C. Each descending level of the WBS does represent an increasingly detailed definition of the project work down to work package level
D. The work breakdown structure is an output of the Create WBS process, not Define Scope.

98: The correct answer is A

A. It is important that the WBS is decomposed down to work package level. The appropriate level of decomposition means that the work package can be reliably estimated in relation to their cost and duration.
B. Activities are work packages that are decomposed further for the purposes of building a project schedule.
C. Elements of the WBS dictionary provide additional information about each work package and not the point in the decomposition of the WBS at which cost and activity durations for the work can be reliably estimated and managed.
D. Tasks is incorrect because it is not part of the standard terminology in the PMBOK® Guide.

99: The correct answer is D

A. Going to far with decomposition means that the benefits derived form the additional work outweigh the costs incurred. This will result in non-productive management effort.
B. Going to far with decomposition means that the benefits derived form the additional work outweigh the costs incurred. These costs will be generated by inefficient use of resources.
C. Going to far with decomposition decrease the ability to get on with doing the actual work.

D. A properly decomposed WBS has the work packages defined at a level where their cost and duration can be accurately estimated and managed. Going beyond this level does not add further benefit or add value and may in fact create adverse results in relation to efficiency and effort.

100: The correct answer is B

A. The WBS does not describe the resources by type. It decomposes the scope statement into work packages.
B. The work breakdown structure organizes and defines the total scope of the project, subdivides the project work into smaller, more manageable pieces, and represents the work specified in the current approved project scope statement. A describes the risk breakdown structure, B describes the resource breakdown structure, and C describes the contract statement of work.
C. The WBS does not define the scope of any contracts. It decomposes the scope statement into work packages.
D. The WBS does not describe project risks. It decomposes the scope statement into work packages.

101: The correct answer is D

A. A fundamental attribute of project management planning is that it will be iterative and subject to rolling wave planning as you can not generally plan the entire project in detail so this approach is not an example of poor project management planning.
B. This answer may seem correct at first glance but it is not a term referenced within the PMBOK® Guide.
C. This answer may seem correct at first glance but it is not a term referenced within the PMBOK® Guide.
D. One important aspect of acknowledging that project planning is iterative and subject to progressive elaborations; work such as decomposition of the WBS may not always be entirely possible as there may be a lack of clarity or a particular deliverable may rely on another deliverable to be complete before it can fully be defined. This process of leaving these uncertain deliverables until more detail is known is called rolling wave planning.

102: The correct answer is B

A. The project charter does not contain enough information to help you gain a more in depth understanding of WBS components.

B. The WBS dictionary is a useful document which lists additional detail about the work packages. Both the project scope statement and the project charter are too high level to provide further detail to work packages contained in the WBS.

C. The project scope statement does not contain enough information to help you gain a more in depth understanding of WBS components.

D. The activity list describes activities not components of the WBS.

103: The correct answer is C

A. This answer is incorrect because scope verification differs from quality control because scope verification means accepting the deliverables match the defined, detailed scope, whereas quality control is concerned with making sure the technical attributes of the product meet the specific quality requirements. Quality control is generally performed before scope verification.

B. This answer is incorrect because scope verification differs from quality control because scope verification means accepting the deliverables match the defined, detailed scope, whereas quality control is concerned with making sure the technical attributes of the product meet the specific quality requirements. Quality control is generally performed before scope verification.

C. Scope verification differs from quality control because scope verification means accepting the deliverables match the defined, detailed scope, whereas quality control is concerned with making sure the technical attributes of the product meet the specific quality requirements. Quality control is generally performed before scope verification.

D. This answer is incorrect because scope verification differs from quality control because scope verification means accepting the deliverables match the defined, detailed scope, whereas quality control is concerned with making sure the technical attributes of the product meet the specific quality requirements. Quality control is generally performed before scope verification.

104: The correct answer is D

A. Accepting approved change requests and amending the project scope baseline is not part of the Validate Scope process.

B. Finalizing the project and product scope statement is the process of Define Scope not the Validate Scope process.

C. Performing variance analysis on the expected and actual deliverables is part of the Monitoring and Controlling process group not the Validate Scope process.

D. The Validate Scope process is the process where you formally check and accept completed project deliverables.

105: The correct answer is A

A. You are completing the Validate Scope process, which is part of the monitoring and controlling process group.

B. This example defines the Validate Scope process, which is part of the monitoring and controlling process group, not work done as part of the Closing process group.

C. This example defines the Validate Scope process, which is part of the monitoring and controlling process group, not work done as part of the Planning process group.

D. This example defines the Validate Scope process, which is part of the monitoring and controlling process group, not work done as part of the Executing process group.

106: The correct answer is A

A. All requests for change to the scope must be considered in light of your agreed integrated change control process. Additionally, as project manager you should proactively influence any prospective change requests.

B. You can not simply refuse to consider change requests but you should always process each change according to your defined change control process.

C. You may do this but only after referring to your change control process for controlling scope and submitting the request as detailed.

D. You may do this but only after referring to your change control process for controlling scope and submitting the request as detailed.

107: The correct answer is C

A. Scope change is part of the formal documented, not undocumented, change process.

B. Scope variance, if it was a real term, would refer to the difference between what your scope baseline is and what you are delivering.
C. Uncontrolled change on a project is a big 'no'. All change must be recorded, documented and assessed as per the integrated change control process. Any approved changes should be reflected in updated baselines.
D. Scope amendment is not a term referenced within the PMBOK® Guide.

108: The correct answer is B

A. The change control plan shows how changes, not requirements, will be managed, assessed and tracked.
B. The requirements management plan documents all aspects of managing, reporting and changing your project requirements.
C. The project management plan is the overall plan comprising all other sub plans including the requirements management plan which is the best answer to this question.
D. The scope management plan sets out how the scope, not the requirements, will be planned, tracked and changed.

109: The correct answer is C

A. Scope baseline analysis is incorrect because it is not a term referenced within the PMBOK® Guide.
B. Change control assessment considers the impact of change requests received not the magnitude of variation from the original scope baseline.
C. You use your project performance measurements to assess the difference between what the scope originally said and what it is now doing. This must always be reflected in the scope baseline.
D. Variation change analysis is incorrect because it is not a term referenced within the PMBOK® Guide.

110: The correct answer is B

A. Quality Control is a quality management process concerned with the correctness and quality of the project deliverables; Validate Scope is concerned with the acceptance of the deliverables against the customer requirements.

B. Quality Control is a quality management process concerned with the correctness and quality of the project deliverables; Validate Scope is concerned with the acceptance of the deliverables against the customer requirements.

C. Quality Control is a quality management process concerned with the correctness and quality of the project deliverables; Validate Scope is concerned with the acceptance of the deliverables against the customer requirements.

D. Quality Control is a quality management process concerned with the correctness and quality of the project deliverables; Validate Scope is concerned with the acceptance of the deliverables against the customer requirements.

111: The correct answer is A

A. If you read the sequence carefully it becomes apparent that each one must precede the next as outputs from one become inputs into the other. You start by defining activities and end by developing the schedule.

B. This answer is incorrect because if you read the sequence carefully it becomes apparent that each one must precede the next as outputs from one become inputs into the other. You start by defining activities and end by developing the schedule. Along the way you first put the defined activities in sequence, then using this information you estimate the activity resources, then you can estimate the activity durations. Some smaller projects may do the activities concurrently.

C. This answer is incorrect because if you read the sequence carefully it becomes apparent that each one must precede the next as outputs from one become inputs into the other. You start by defining activities and end by developing the schedule. D. This answer is incorrect because if you read the sequence carefully it becomes apparent that each one must precede the next as outputs from one become inputs into the other. You start by defining activities and end by developing the schedule.

112: The correct answer is D

A. Work package assignments refer to the resources allocated to complete the work packages.

B. Project tasks is an informal term used by some project managers. For the purpose of the exam the correct term to use is activities.

C. WBS dictionary items provide more detailed information about each node of the WBS. They do not refer to any work below the level of work package.

D. When you developed your WBS your process of decomposition went down to a level where the element of the scope could be accurately estimated for duration and cost. The next step in the decomposition process is to break it down into activities which represe

113: The correct answer is A

A. Involving the people who will actually be responsible for completing the work will result in more accurate information. It is not certain the involvement of team members will add extra cost to the project as you are not given enough information to decide

B. This answer is incorrect because involving the people who will actually be responsible for completing the work will result in more accurate information leading to greater efficiencies.

C. This answer is incorrect because involving the people who will actually be responsible for completing the work will result in greater morale as people feel valued.

D. This answer is incorrect because involving the people who will actually be responsible for completing the work will result in more accurate information.

114: The correct answer is A

A. The milestone list would be found in your WBS dictionary.

B. The scope of work description is contained in the activity list.

C. All schedule activities required on the project are contained in the activity list.

D. Activity identifiers are contained in the activity list.

115: The correct answer is A

A. Did you read this question properly? Did you notice that there is a start-to-start relationship between task D and task C? Since Task D is dependent upon Task C starting and not finishing, the critical path of the project is D-E-F, which has a duration of 13 days

B. *Did you read this question properly? Did you notice that there is a start-to-start relationship between task D and task C? Since Task D is dependent upon Task C starting and not finishing, the critical path of the project is D-E-F, which has a duration of 13 days.*
C. *Did you read this question properly? Did you notice that there is a start-to-start relationship between task D and task C? Since Task D is dependent upon Task C starting and not finishing, the critical path of the project is D-E-F, which has a duration of 13 days*
D. *Did you read this question properly? Did you notice that there is a start-to-start relationship between task D and task C? Since Task D is dependent upon Task C starting and not finishing, the critical path of the project is D-E-F, which has a duration of13 days*

116: The correct answer is B

A. *Very few activities have start-to -finish relationships which means that the successor activity can't finish until its predecessor activity starts.*
B. *Finish-to-start means that the successor activity can't start until its predecessor activity is finished. Most activities have this sort of relationship. Very few have start-to -finish relationships which means that the successor activity cant finish until its predecessor activity starts.*
C. *Finish-to-finish is often used but it is not the most common type of relationship.*
D. *Start-to-start is often used but it is not the most common type of relationship.*

117: The correct answer is C

A. *Critical chain methodology refers to a process of including buffers throughout the schedule to deal with bottlenecks and uncertainty.*
B. *Activity on arrow diagrams are referred to as arrow diagramming methods, not precedence diagramming methods.*
C. *The activity on node diagram is called this because the activity and information about the activity is shown on a node in the diagram represented by a square or rectangle. Relationship between nodes is shown by arrows.*
D. *The precedence diagramming method can be used as part of the critical path methodology but the correct answer is activity on node.*

118: The correct answer is C

A. Slack refers to the amount of time that an activity can be delayed before it impacts upon successor activities start dates. It is one of the few instances in the PMBOK® Guide where two terms, slack and float, are interchangeable.

B. Lag refers to the amount of time a successor activity must wait after the end of its predecessor before it can start.

C. A lead means that one activity can get a start on its predecessor finishing. Even through it has a finish-to-start relationship it can start prior to the predecessor finishing. It would be shown on a network diagram as having a finish-to-start relationship

D. Float refers to the amount of time that an activity can be delayed before it impacts upon successor activities start dates. It is one of the few instances in the PMBOK® Guide where two terms, slack and float, are interchangeable.

119: The correct answer is A

A. A lead means that one activity can get a start on its predecessor finishing. Even through it has a finish-to-start relationship it can start prior to the predecessor finishing. It would be shown on a network diagram as having a finish-to-start relationshi

B. This answer is incorrect because a lead means that one activity can get a start on its predecessor finishing. Even through it has a finish-to-start relationship it can start prior to the predecessor finishing. It would be shown on a network diagram as having a finish-to-start relationship with a certain lead time. A lag on the other hand is a delay between related activities.

C. This answer is incorrect because a lead means that one activity can get a start on its predecessor finishing. Even through it has a finish-to-start relationship it can start prior to the predecessor finishing.

D. This answer is incorrect because a lead means that one activity can get a start on its predecessor finishing. Even through it has a finish-to-start relationship it can start prior to the predecessor finishing.

120: The correct answer is B

A. A discretionary dependency is one where a successor should come after the predecessor but there is some discretion particular if a schedule requires compression to shorten duration.

B. An external dependency means that you are waiting on work being done by people or organizations outside of the project.
C. There is no such term as environmental dependency in the PMBOK® Guide
D. A mandatory dependency means that the successor must come after the predecessor. A mandatory dependency is also one which is internal, not external, to the project.

121: The correct answer is A

A. The first iteration of the project network schedule diagram is an output of the Sequence activities process.
B. The Define Activities process produces the activity list as its primary output.
C. The Develop Schedule process produces the schedule baseline as its primary output.
D. The Control Schedule process produces work performance information as its primary output.

122: The correct answer is B

A. The dates of annual holidays for project team members would be a part of the information included in the resource calendar but it is not the best answer available.
B. Your resource calendar is a useful input into the Estimate Activity Resources process at it clearly shows when and where resources will be available to the project.
C. The resource calendar does not show the duration of each activity. This would be shown in the network schedule.
D. The length of time the project will require input from external resources Is not shown in the resource calendar. This would be part of the information shown in the network schedule.

123: The correct answer is A

A. There are a number of ways to complete an estimating process. When an activity can not be estimated with a reasonable degree of confidence, the work within it is decomposed further down to its lowest level and the resource needs are then estimated. aggreg

B. Published estimating data is a database of data about costs and quantities.

C. Expert judgment is not the correct answer because it uses the experience of experts to help your estimating process.

D. Parametric estimating is a process that multiplies known quantities by known financial rates.

124: The correct answer is D

A. The Estimate Activity Durations process has many inputs and the activity list is one of them.

B. The Estimate Activity Durations process has many inputs and activity attributes is one of them.

C. The Estimate Activity Durations process has many inputs and the project scope statement is one of them.

D. Activity Duration Estimates is an output, not an input, of Estimate Activity Duration the process.

125: The correct answer is A

A. Analogous estimating involves using information from similar projects (i.e. an analogy) to estimate elements of your project and is generally less costly and time consuming than other techniques.

B. This is not an example of bottom-up estimating. Bottom-up estimating breaks down work packages and activities into the smallest possible piece of work then adds up the time and cost for each to get a total project cost or duration

C. This is not an example of parametric estimating. Parametric estimating is a process that multiplies known quantities by known financial rates.

D. This is not an example of three point estimating. Three point estimating uses the optimistic, realistic and pessimistic estimates to calculate a weight average.

126: The correct answer is D

A. Using three point estimating the expected duration is: (6+(8x4)+16)/6 = 9 days.

B. Using three point estimating the expected duration is: (6+(8x4)+16)/6 = 9 days.

C. Using three point estimating the expected duration is: (6+(8x4)+16)/6
= 9 days.
D. Using three point estimating the expected duration is: (6+(8x4)+16)/6
= 9 days.

127: The correct answer is D

A. This is not an example of parametric estimating. Parametric estimating
is a process that multiplies known quantities by known financial rates.
B. This is not an example of bottom-up estimating. Bottom-up estimating
breaks down work packages and activities into the smallest possible piece of
work then adds up the time and cost for each to get a total project cost or
duration
C. This is not an example of analogous estimating. Analogous estimating
involves using information from similar projects (i.e. an analogy) to
estimate elements of your project and is generally less costly and time
consuming than other techniques.
D. Three point estimating, or PERT analysis, uses a weighted average
method with emphasis given to the most likely data, to estimate a duration.

128: The correct answer is A

A. Parametric estimating uses numbers and quantifiable measures to
estimate. Remember if you see the word 'metric' it means number of
measure.
B. This is not an example of bottom-up estimating. Bottom-up estimating
breaks down work packages and activities into the smallest possible piece of
work then adds up the time and cost for each to get a total project cost or
duration
C. This is not an example of analogous estimating. Analogous estimating
involves using information from similar projects (i.e. an analogy) to
estimate elements of your project and is generally less costly and time
consuming than other techniques.
D. This is not an example of three point estimating. Three point estimating
uses the optimistic, realistic and pessimistic estimates to calculate a weight
average.

129: The correct answer is B

A. There are many inputs into the Develop Schedule process and project schedule network diagrams is one of them.
B. The project schedule is an output from the Develop Schedule process.
C. There are many inputs into the Develop Schedule process and the activity list is one of them.
D. There are many inputs into the Develop Schedule process and resource calendar is one of them.

130: The correct answer is C

A. Project schedule development is not the name of a PMBOK® Guide process.
B. Create project schedule is not the name of a PMBOK® Guide process.
C. This is the final stage in the planning process group for the time management knowledge area. It takes all the previous information from the previous planning processes and makes the project schedule.
D. Schedule management is not the name of a PMBOK® Guide process.

131: The correct answer is C

A. This question requires you to draw a network diagram. The duration of the project is represented by completing a forward pass over the network diagram. In this case once you have drawn the network diagram you would see that the duration of the project is 15 days.
B. This question requires you to draw a network diagram. The duration of the project is represented by completing a forward pass over the network diagram. In this case once you have drawn the network diagram you would see that the duration of the project is 15 days.
C. This question requires you to draw a network diagram. The duration of the project is represented by completing a forward pass over the network diagram. In this case once you have drawn the network diagram you would see that the duration of the project is 15 days.
D. This question requires you to draw a network diagram. The duration of the project is represented by completing a forward pass over the network diagram. In this case once you have drawn the network diagram you would see that the duration of the project is 15 days.

132: The correct answer is C

A. The critical path is obtained after you have completed both a forward pass and backward pass over the network diagram. In this instance that forward pass revealed a duration of 15 days and the critical path is Start-B-D-E-Finish. Activities on the critica

B. The critical path is obtained after you have completed both a forward pass and backward pass over the network diagram. In this instance that forward pass revealed a duration of 15 days and the critical path is Start-B-D-E-Finish. Activities on the critical path have no float in them so that any delays on the critical directly impact on the project duration.

C. The critical path is obtained after you have completed both a forward pass and backward pass over the network diagram. In this instance that forward pass revealed a duration of 15 days and the critical path is Start-B-D-E-Finish.

D. The critical path is obtained after you have completed both a forward pass and backward pass over the network diagram. In this instance that forward pass revealed a duration of 15 days and the critical path is Start-B-D-E-Finish.

133: The correct answer is C

A. In critical chain theory the feeder chains are activities that are not on the critical path. These tasks are scheduled to be done as late as possible and then buffered so that they start earlier than the late schedule dates.

B. In critical chain theory the feeder chains are activities that are not on the critical path. These tasks are scheduled to be done as late as possible and then buffered so that they start earlier than the late schedule dates. Buffer is also added to the critical path of the schedule to improve the probability that the project will finish on time. Feeder chain activities as well as critical chain activities are not started as early as possible or as late as possible. They are started as late as possible minus their buffer.

C. In critical chain theory the feeder chains are activities that are not on the critical path. These tasks are scheduled to be done as late as possible and then buffered so that they start earlier than the late schedule dates.

D. In critical chain theory the feeder chains are activities that are not on the critical path. These tasks are scheduled to be done as late as possible and then buffered so that they start earlier than the late schedule dates.

134: The correct answer is B

A. Both methods seek to use accurate estimates.

B. Both the critical path method and the critical chain method accounts for resource availability.

C. This answer is incorrect because the critical path method is not just focused on managing the total float of network paths .

D. This answer is incorrect because the critical chain method does not schedule only late start dates to planned activities.

135: The correct answer is A

A. The critical chain method is a schedule network analysis technique that modifies a project schedule to account for limited resources by deliberately adding in non working time buffers which is intended to protect the target finish date form slippage along

B. The critical path method does not add in buffers between activities.

C. Three point estimating uses the pessimistic, realistic and optimistic estimates to get a weight average.

D. Parametric estimating is a process that multiplies known quantities by known financial rates.

136: The correct answer is B

A. The critical chain method is a schedule network analysis technique that modifies a project schedule to account for limited resources by deliberately adding in non working time buffers which is intended to protect the target finish date from slippage along

B. Critical Path methodology focuses on the amount of float in network paths to determine the critical path through a project. The critical path has no float associated with it and as such represents the greatest risk to the project duration.

C. Parametric estimating is a process that multiplies known quantities by known financial rates.

D. Three point estimating uses the pessimistic, realistic and optimistic estimates to get a weight average.

137: The correct answer is C

A. The number of resources required does not generally change during a first attempt at resource leveling. It is more likely the duration will increase.

B. The number of resources required does not generally change during a first attempt at resource leveling. It is more likely the duration will increase.
C. The logical analysis of the schedule often produces a preliminary schedule that requires more resources during certain time periods than are available, or requires changes in resource levels that are not manageable. Heuristics such as "allocate scarce re
D. The first attempt at resource leveling generally increases, not decreases, the project duration due to the reallocation of resources and the consequences on the timing of the work being done.

138: The correct answer is A

A. The person who is working on the task that has free float of five days can be used on the task that is in trouble for five days without affecting the other task schedules in the project.
B. The person who is working on the task that has free float of five days can be used on the task that is in trouble for five days without affecting the other task schedules in the project. The person working on the task that has total float of eight days can be used on the task that is in trouble, but since there is zero free float for this task, there will have to be a rescheduling of other tasks to allow this.
C. The person who is working on the task that has free float of five days can be used on the task that is in trouble for five days without affecting the other task schedules in the project.
D. The person who is working on the task that has free float of five days can be used on the task that is in trouble for five days without affecting the other task schedules in the project.

139: The correct answer is C

A. The critical chain method is a schedule network analysis technique that modifies a project schedule to account for limited resources by deliberately adding in non working time buffers which is intended to protect the target finish date from slippage along the way
B. Schedule compression involves using fast-tracking or crashing to reduce the project duration.

C. A What-if Scenario analysis runs through all the different outcomes if a particular scenario occurs. This level of information can assist with many types of estimating to get the full range of possibilities. The most comprehensive type of What-if Scenario

D. This is not an example of parametric estimating. Parametric estimating is a process that multiplies known quantities by known financial rates.

140: The correct answer is B

A. Compressing is not the correct answer as it is a generic term for all schedule compression techniques

B. Crashing a project schedule involves bringing in more resource to do the work. Extra resource usually costs more money. Fast tracking on the other hand involves completing activities in parallel that might normally be done in sequence. This does not always cost more money.

C. Fast tracking is a schedule compression technique but one that programs activities in parallel instead of in sequence. Crashing is the other main schedule compression technique and it uses extra budget to provide more resources.

D. Resource leveling is not the correct answer because it focuses on getting an optimal allocation of resources across the project.

141: The correct answer is D

A. Crashing a project schedule involves bringing in more resource to do the work. Extra resource usually costs more money. Fast tracking on the other hand involves completing activities in parallel that might normally be done in sequence.

B. Increasing priorities will not change the order in which work has to be done nor the duration.

C. This may seem like you are accelerating the project schedule but the correct term to use is fast tracking.

D. Fast tracking a schedule is finding activities that can be done in parallel that were originally scheduled to be done in sequence.

142: The correct answer is D

A. Resource leveling is not the correct answer because it focuses on getting an optimal allocation of resources across the project.

B. Compressing is not the correct answer as it is a generic term for all schedule compression techniques

C. Crashing a project schedule involves bringing in more resource to do the work. Extra resource usually costs more money. Fast tracking on the other hand involves completing activities in parallel that might normally be done in sequence. This does not alway

D. Fast tracking means running activities that might normally be run in sequence in parallel. It does not normally incur extra cost.

143: The correct answer is C

A. Work performance information not be the best answer because it contains far too much detail to communicate effectively in this situation.

B. The project management plan would not be the best answer because it contains far too much detail to communicate effectively in this situation.

C. The question sets out that it is senior management and you only have a short amount of time therefore you want to present only high level information about the project. A bar chart, such as a Gantt chart does this very well.

D. The schedule network diagram would not be the best answer because it contains far too much detail to communicate effectively in this situation.

144: The correct answer is C

A. This answer is not correct because it is a made up process name.

B. Monitoring and Controlling is a process group not an individual process.

C. Control Schedule is the only time management knowledge area process that appears in the monitoring and controlling process group.

D. The Develop Schedule process produces the project schedule and schedule baseline.

145: The correct answer is C

A. The Control Schedule process has several inputs and the project schedule is one of them

B. The Control Schedule process has several inputs and the project management plan is one of them

C. This is a tricky question that requires you to know the difference between inputs and outputs. Work performance information such as the calculated SV and SPI values for WBS components are outputs on the Control Schedule process.

D. The Control Schedule process has several inputs and work performance data is one of them

146: The correct answer is C

A. This calculation does not immediately tell you if your amount of buffer is less than optimal

B. This calculation does not immediately tell you if your network diagram was incorrectly put together.

C. An SPI of 1 means the project is on schedule, less that 1 means behind schedule and greater than 1 means ahead of schedule.

D. This answer is incorrect because an SPI of 1 means the project is on schedule, less that 1 means behind schedule and greater than 1 means ahead of schedule.

147: The correct answer is A

A. To get this answer you need to work backwards from the normal equations for calculating SPI. In this case then the value equals $10,000 divided by .95 which equals $10,526.

B. To get this answer you need to work backwards from the normal equations for calculating SPI. In this case then the value equals $10,000 divided by .95 which equals $10,526.

C. To get this answer you need to work backwards from the normal equations for calculating SPI. In this case then the value equals $10,000 divided by .95 which equals $10,526.

D. To get this answer you need to work backwards from the normal equations for calculating SPI. In this case then the value equals $10,000 divided by .95 which equals $10,526.

148: The correct answer is A

A. For the PMP® exam you will need to know how to calculate standard deviation and variance by simply means. In this case Standard Deviation = $(P-O)/6$.

B. For the PMP® exam you will need to know how to calculate standard deviation and variance by simply means. In this case Standard Deviation = (P-O)/6.

C. For the PMP® exam you will need to know how to calculate standard deviation and variance by simply means. In this case Standard Deviation = (P-O)/6.

D. For the PMP® exam you will need to know how to calculate standard deviation and variance by simply means. In this case Standard Deviation = (P-O)/6.

149: The correct answer is C

A. The 95% confidence interval is two standard deviations either side of the mean. We know the mean =10.33 and the standard deviation equals 1.33 so the duration range that we are 95% confident about is:10.33±(2*1.33).

B. The 95% confidence interval is two standard deviations either side of the mean. We know the mean =10.33 and the standard deviation equals 1.33 so the duration range that we are 95% confident about is:10.33±(2*1.33).

C. The 95% confidence interval is two standard deviations either side of the mean. We know the mean =10.33 and the standard deviation equals 1.33 so the duration range that we are 95% confident about is:10.33±(2*1.33).

D. The 95% confidence interval is two standard deviations either side of the mean. We know the mean =10.33 and the standard deviation equals 1.33 so the duration range that we are 95% confident about is:10.33±(2*1.33).

150: The correct answer is B

A. Analogous estimate use an analogy from a previous project and extrapolate from that an estimate for a current project. The question presents an example of parametric estimating.

B. Parametric estimating is an estimating technique that uses a statistical relationship between historical data and other variables to calculate an estimate for activity parameters.

C. Three point estimating uses the pessimistic, realistic and optimistic estimates to get a weight average.

D. Expert judgment uses the experience of experts to assist in preparing estimates.

151: The correct answer is A

A. Once you have compiled information in the question into a table that lists task ID, duration and predecessors you to map out a network diagram that shows that the critical path is A-B-C-E-F-G.

B. Once you have compiled information in the question into a table that lists task ID, duration and predecessors you to map out a network diagram that shows that the critical path is A-B-C-E-F-G. This one may have taken you quite a while to work out and, if you get a question such as this in the exam you must remember that every question is worth one point in the time taken to answer this question you could have answered several other questions.

C. Once you have compiled information in the question into a table that lists task ID, duration and predecessors you to map out a network diagram that shows that the critical path is A-B-C-E-F-G.

D. Once you have compiled information in the question into a table that lists task ID, duration and predecessors you to map out a network diagram that shows that the critical path is A-B-C-E-F-G.

152: The correct answer is A

A. Once you have compiled information in the question into a table that lists task ID, duration and predecessors you to map out a network diagram that shows that the critical path is A-B-C-E-F-G and that only task D has slack of two days.

B. Once you have compiled information in the question into a table that lists task ID, duration and predecessors you to map out a network diagram that shows that the critical path is A-B-C-E-F-G and that only task D has slack of two days. This one may have taken you quite a while to work out and, if you get a question such as this in the exam you must remember that every question is worth one point in the time taken to answer this question you could have answered several other questions.

C. Once you have compiled information in the question into a table that lists task ID, duration and predecessors you to map out a network diagram that shows that the critical path is A-B-C-E-F-G and that only task D has slack of two days.

D. Once you have compiled information in the question into a table that lists task ID, duration and predecessors you to map out a network diagram that shows that the critical path is A-B-C-E-F-G and that only task D has slack of two days.

153: The correct answer is A

A. This description matches the PMBOK® Guide description of the Determine Budget process.
B. The Estimate Costs process does not aggregate individual cost estimates.
C. The Control Costs process monitors and controls change to the costs estimates and project budget and does not aggregate individual cost estimates.
D. The cost performance baseline is an output not a process.

154: The correct answer is C

A. The cost management plan establishes several things relating to costs on the project and the units of measure is one of these.
B. The cost management plan establishes several things relating to costs on the project and the level of accuracy is one of these.
C. Activity definition is performed during the project schedule management processes.
D. The cost management plan establishes several things relating to costs on the project and the control thresholds is one of these.

155: The correct answer is A

A. Costs that are directly attributable to a project are known as direct costs. Costs such as organization overheads, that are spread over several projects are known as indirect costs.
B. Costs that are directly attributable to a project are known as direct costs. Costs such as organization overheads, that are spread over several projects are known as indirect costs.
C. This answer is not correct because it is not a term referenced within the PMBOK® Guide.
D. This answer is not correct because it is not a term referenced within the PMBOK® Guide.

156: The correct answer is B

A. The Estimate Costs process has several inputs and the project schedule is one of these.
B. Activity cost estimates is the output from the Estimate Costs process.
C. The Estimate Costs process has several inputs and the risk register is one of these.
D. The Estimate Costs process has several inputs and the scope baseline is one of these.

157: The correct answer is D

A. There are many organizational process assets you could use when estimating costs and any lessons learned database your organization has would be one of these.
B. There are many organizational process assets you could use when estimating costs and cost estimating templates your organization has would be one of these.
C. There are many organizational process assets you could use when estimating costs and any historical information your organization has would be one of these.
D. Market considerations are an example of an enterprise environmental factor not an organizational process asset.

158: The correct answer is C

A. Three point estimating uses the pessimistic, realistic and optimistic estimates to get a weight average.
B. Parametric estimating is a process that multiplies known quantities by known financial rates.
C. Analogous estimating is used several times as a tool and technique in different estimating areas throughout the PMBOK® Guide.
D. Published estimating data is a database of data about costs and quantities.

159: The correct answer is C

A. Low level estimating may sound correct but it is not a term referenced within the PMBOK® Guide.

B. Parametric estimating is an estimating technique that uses a statistical relationship between historical data and other variables to calculate an estimate for activity parameters.
C. Bottom-up estimating is a technique for estimating the cost of individual work packages with the lowest level of detail.
D. Project management software may be useful for developing cost estimates but it is a tool not a technique.

160: The correct answer is C

A. This answer is incorrect because it is not a term referenced within the PMBOK® Guide.
B. Bottom-up estimating is a technique for estimating the cost of individual work packages with the lowest level of detail.
C. Parametric estimating is a technique that uses a statistical relationship between historical data and other variables to calculate a cost estimate for a schedule activity resource.
D. Top-down estimating is a macro estimating technique that assigns costs to particular deliverables and work packages.

161: The correct answer is B

A. Parametric estimating requires access to estimating databases and as such is generally more costly that analogous estimating.
B. Analogous estimating is generally less costly than other estimating techniques but also generally less accurate.
C. Resource rate estimating is not correct because it is a made-up term.
D. Bottom-up estimating is not correct because of the time and cost involved in decomposing the WBS means that it is more costly than analogous estimating.

162: The correct answer is B

A. The three point estimating technique, or PERT analysis, uses a weighted average method to arrive at what should be a more accurate estimate. In this case the correct answer is $(15+(4x25)+70)/6 = 30.83$.
B. The three point estimating technique, or PERT analysis, uses a weighted average method to arrive at what should be a more accurate estimate. In this case the correct answer is $(15+(4x25)+70)/6 = 30.83$.

C. The three point estimating technique, or PERT analysis, uses a weighted average method to arrive at what should be a more accurate estimate. In this case the correct answer is (15+(4x25)+70)/6 = 30.83.
D. The three point estimating technique, or PERT analysis, uses a weighted average method to arrive at what should be a more accurate estimate. In this case the correct answer is (15+(4x25)+70)/6 = 30.83.

163: The correct answer is A

A. The three point estimating technique, or PERT analysis, uses a weighted average method to arrive at what should be a more accurate estimate. In this case the correct answer is (30+(4x50)+70)/6 = 50.
B. The three point estimating technique, or PERT analysis, uses a weighted average method to arrive at what should be a more accurate estimate. In this case the correct answer is (30+(4x50)+70)/6 = 50.
C. The three point estimating technique, or PERT analysis, uses a weighted average method to arrive at what should be a more accurate estimate. In this case the correct answer is (30+(4x50)+70)/6 = 50.
D. The three point estimating technique, or PERT analysis, uses a weighted average method to arrive at what should be a more accurate estimate. In this case the correct answer is (30+(4x50)+70)/6 = 50.

164: The correct answer is A

A. When you are preparing estimates generally there are still a few unknowns in the project and it is wise to include a contingency reserve as part of your project budget. This can be reduced or given up as the project progresses and more information is know
B. Reserve analysis is the process of deciding what sort of reserve you need and once agreed upon, reexamining it to make sure it is still appropriate.
C. Management reserve is a fund held by management for unforeseen risks that emerge on projects. It is not generally calculated for individual projects.
D. Slush fund is an informal name sometimes given to management reserves.

165: The correct answer is C

A. In the three point estimating calculation the standard deviation is calculated by squaring the standard deviation for each of the activities on the critical path of the project, adding them together, and then taking the square root.

B. In the three point estimating calculation the standard deviation is calculated by squaring the standard deviation for each of the activities on the critical path of the project, adding them together, and then taking the square root. This is the standard deviation of the project. Plus or minus two standard deviations from the expected value of the project duration will have a range of values such that the project has a 95% probability of actually finishing within the dates calculated. So to get the answer you first get the square root of 14 which is 4. The multiply this by 2 to get 8, then add 8, and subtract 8 from the mean of 90.

C. In the three point estimating calculation the standard deviation is calculated by squaring the standard deviation for each of the activities on the critical path of the project, adding them together, and then taking the square root.

D. In the three point estimating calculation the standard deviation is calculated by squaring the standard deviation for each of the activities on the critical path of the project, adding them together, and then taking the square root.

166: The correct answer is D

A. The cost performance baseline is not a PMBOK® Guide process.

B. Budget preparation is not a PMBOK® Guide process.

C. The Estimate costs process develops individual cost estimates which are then aggregating over time in the Determine Budget process to establish an authorized cost baseline.

D. Once you have done all your costs estimating you can then add them all together to get a cost baseline; this is known as Determine Budget process. Although represented as sequential processes they may be done concurrently.

167: The correct answer is B

A. The basis of estimates is an input into the Determine Budget process.

B. The cost baseline is an output of the Determine Budget process.

C. Activity cost estimates are an input into the Determine Budget process.

D. The scope baseline is an input into the Determine Budget process.

168: The correct answer is A

A. The cost baseline is the aggregation of your Estimate Cost and Determine Budget processes.
B. The approved project budget may sound like a correct term but it is not the one that is in the PMBOK® Guide.
C. Activity cost estimates are an input into the Determine Budget process and they become the cost baseline once amalgamated with elements of the schedule.
D. Total funding requirements may sound like a correct term but it is not the one that is in the PMBOK® Guide.

169: The correct answer is A

A. The process of controlling costs is one of the more technical processes to understand for the PMP® exam as it includes the earned value tools and techniques.
B. Determine Budget develops the project cost baseline which is then monitored during the Control Costs process.
C. Earned value management is not a process but a tool that can be used during the Control Costs process
D. Cost aggregation is when you add all your individual cost estimates together. It is not a monitoring and controlling process

170: The correct answer is A

A. Work performance information is an input to the Control Cost process. All the other 3 are key dimensions of the Earned Value Management tool.
B. Earned value is the value of the work actually performed and is a key element in earned value management.
C. Planned value is the planned value of work performed and is a key element in earned value management.
D. Actual cost is what is cost to do the work performed and is a key element in earned value management.

171: The correct answer is A

A. A positive schedule variance means you are achieving ahead of your baseline, so feel free to congratulate your team. Remember that you must always be delivering to the agreed documentation including the relevant baseline documents. As such you will need t

B. You don't need to crash the schedule as a positive schedule variance means you are ahead of time.

C. You don't need to fast track the schedule as a positive schedule variance means you are ahead of time.

D. You are doing well but you must process the variance through your agreed change control process.

172: The correct answer is C

A. Schedule variance (SV) = Earned Value (V) - Planned value (PV), so $SV = 15,000-20,000 = -5,000$.

B. Schedule variance (SV) = Earned Value (V) - Planned value (PV), so $SV = 15,000-20,000 = -5,000$.

C. Schedule variance (SV) = Earned Value (V) - Planned value (PV), so $SV = 15,000-20,000 = -5,000$.

D. Schedule variance (SV) = Earned Value (V) - Planned value (PV), so $SV = 15,000-20,000 = -5,000$.

173: The correct answer is C

A. Cost variance (SV)= Earned Value (EV) - Actual Costs (AC), so $CV = 18,000-15,000 = 3,000$.

B. Cost variance (SV)= Earned Value (EV) - Actual Costs (AC), so $CV = 18,000-15,000 = 3,000$.

C. Cost variance (SV)= Earned Value (EV) - Actual Costs (AC), so $CV = 18,000-15,000 = 3,000$.

D. Cost variance (SV)= Earned Value (EV) - Actual Costs (AC), so $CV = 18,000-15,000 = 3,000$.

174: The correct answer is B

A. Schedule variance (SV) = Earned Value (EV) - Planned value (PV), so $SV = 26,000-20,000 = 6,000$.

B. Schedule variance (SV) = Earned Value (EV) - Planned value (PV), so $SV = 26,000-20,000 = 6,000$.

C. Schedule variance (SV) = Earned Value (EV) - Planned value (PV), so SV = 26,000-20,000 = 6,000.

D. Schedule variance (SV) = Earned Value (EV) - Planned value (PV), so SV = 26,000-20,000 = 6,000.

175: The correct answer is D

A. Cost variance (SV) = Earned Value (EV) - Actual Costs (AC), so CV = 52,000-49,000 = 3,000.

B. Cost variance (SV) = Earned Value (EV) - Actual Costs (AC), so CV = 52,000-49,000 = 3,000.

C. Cost variance (SV) = Earned Value (EV) - Actual Costs (AC), so CV = 52,000-49,000 = 3,000.

D. Cost variance (SV) = Earned Value (EV) - Actual Costs (AC), so CV = 52,000-49,000 = 3,000.

176: The correct answer is A

A. Budget at completion (BAC) is the total planned value (PV) for the project.

B. The cost baseline represents the approved budget for the project

C. Actual cost is what is cost to do the work performed and is a key element in earned value management.

D. The approved project budget is more correctly called the cost baseline.

177: The correct answer is D

A. Budget at completion (BAC) is the total planned value (PV) for the project.

B. The cost baseline represents the approved budget for the project

C. Actual cost is what is cost to do the work performed and is a key element in earned value management.

D. Earned value measures what work you have actually completed and compares this to the actual costs of completing the work. When compared to the planned value of the project at the given point in time you are able to see if the project is on track or not.

178: The correct answer is D

A. The percent complete is the work completed, or the earned value divided by the total work to be done. EV / BAC = 24 / 97 = 25%.
B. The percent complete is the work completed, or the earned value divided by the total work to be done. EV / BAC = 24 / 97 = 25%.
C. The percent complete is the work completed, or the earned value divided by the total work to be done. EV / BAC = 24 / 97 = 25%.
D. The percent complete is the work completed, or the earned value divided by the total work to be done. EV / BAC = 24 / 97 = 25%.

179: The correct answer is B

A. The formula for Cost Variance is CV = EV - AC. Therefore if CV = $50,000 and EV = $125,000, then AC must equal $75,000.
B. The formula for Cost Variance is CV = EV - AC. Therefore if CV = $50,000 and EV = $125,000, then AC must equal $75,000.
C. The formula for Cost Variance is CV = EV - AC. Therefore if CV = $50,000 and EV = $125,000, then AC must equal $75,000.
D. The formula for Cost Variance is CV = EV - AC. Therefore if CV = $50,000 and EV = $125,000, then AC must equal $75,000.

180: The correct answer is C

A. 1.11 is not correct
B. 0.9 is not correct
C. This question requires you to work out the Earned Value (EV) by determining what EV will give an SPI of 1.1 if the PV is $5 000. To calculate this you need to divide the SPI by the PV which will give you an earned value (EV) of $5 500. You can then calcul
D. 1.0 is not correct

181: The correct answer is B

A. Schedule Performance index (SPI) = Earned Value (EV) / Planned Value (PV), so SPI = 20000/25000 = 0.8.
B. Schedule Performance index (SPI) = Earned Value (EV) / Planned Value (PV), so SPI = 20000/25000 = 0.8.
C. Schedule Performance index (SPI) = Earned Value (EV) / Planned Value (PV), so SPI = 20000/25000 = 0.8.
D. Schedule Performance index (SPI) = Earned Value (EV) / Planned Value (PV), so SPI = 20000/25000 = 0.8.

182: The correct answer is D

A. Schedule Performance index (SPI) = Earned Value (EV) / Planned Value (PV), so SPI = 25,000/20,000 = 1.25.
B. Schedule Performance index (SPI) = Earned Value (EV) / Planned Value (PV), so SPI = 25,000/20,000 = 1.25.
C. Schedule Performance index (SPI) = Earned Value (EV) / Planned Value (PV), so SPI = 25,000/20,000 = 1.25.
D. Schedule Performance index (SPI) = Earned Value (EV) / Planned Value (PV), so SPI = 25,000/20,000 = 1.25.

183: The correct answer is A

A. Cost performance index (CPI) = Earned Value (EV) / Actual Cost (AC), so CPI = 100,000/90,000 = 1.11.
B. Cost performance index (CPI) = Earned Value (EV) / Actual Cost (AC), so CPI = 100,000/90,000 = 1.11.
C. Cost performance index (CPI) = Earned Value (EV) / Actual Cost (AC), so CPI = 100,000/90,000 = 1.11.
D. Cost performance index (CPI) = Earned Value (EV) / Actual Cost (AC), so CPI = 100,000/90,000 = 1.11.

184: The correct answer is A

A. Cost performance index (CPI) = Earned Value (EV) / Actual Cost (AC), so CPI = 9,000/8,000 = 1.125.
B. Cost performance index (CPI) = Earned Value (EV) / Actual Cost (AC), so CPI = 9,000/8,000 = 1.125.
C. Cost performance index (CPI) = Earned Value (EV) / Actual Cost (AC), so CPI = 9,000/8,000 = 1.125.
D. Cost performance index (CPI) = Earned Value (EV) / Actual Cost (AC), so CPI = 9,000/8,000 = 1.125.

185: The correct answer is C

A. The formula for Cost Variance is CV = EV - AC. Therefore if CV = $50,000 and EV = $125,000, then AC must equal $75,000. The formula for CPI is CPI = EV / AC. Therefore CPI = $125,000 / $75,000 or 1.66.

B. The formula for Cost Variance is CV = EV - AC. Therefore if CV = $50,000 and EV = $125,000, then AC must equal $75,000. The formula for CPI is CPI = EV / AC. Therefore CPI = $125,000 / $75,000 or 1.66.
C. The formula for Cost Variance is CV = EV - AC. Therefore if CV = $50,000 and EV = $125,000, then AC must equal $75,000. The formula for CPI is CPI = EV / AC. Therefore CPI = $125,000 / $75,000 or 1.66.
D. The formula for Cost Variance is CV = EV - AC. Therefore if CV = $50,000 and EV = $125,000, then AC must equal $75,000. The formula for CPI is CPI = EV / AC. Therefore CPI = $125,000 / $75,000 or 1.66.

186: The correct answer is A

A. A CPI below 1 tells you that you are experiencing a cost overrun on the project. This is true for the SPI measurement as well.
B. A CPI of 0.89 means that for every dollar you are spending you are getting 89 cents of value.
C. A CPI below 1 tells you that you are experiencing a cost overrun on the project. This is true for the SPI measurement as well.
D. The CPI tells you about cost performance only and can not tell you anything about schedule performance.

187: The correct answer is C

A. A CPI above 1 means a cost underrun, while an SPI below 1 means you are not achieving all the work you had planned within the timeframe you are measuring.
B. A CPI above 1 means a cost underrun, while an SPI below 1 means you are not achieving all the work you had planned within the timeframe you are measuring.
C. A CPI above 1 means a cost underrun, while an SPI below 1 means you are not achieving all the work you had planned within the timeframe you are measuring.
D. A CPI above 1 means a cost underrun, while an SPI below 1 means you are not achieving all the work you had planned within the timeframe you are measuring.

188: The correct answer is A

A. Bottom-up estimating is a technique for estimating the cost of individual work packages with the lowest level of detail and as such it incurs extra costs because of the effort involved.

B. Earned value management is a valuable technique for assessing any cost and schedule variances.

C. The estimate to complete (ETC) forecast does not require as much effort nor incur as many costs as bottom-up estimating techniques.

D. The to complete performance index (TCPI) measures the rate at which you must go to achieve either the EAC or BAC.

189: The correct answer is C

A. In this instance with the information provided you are being lead to use $EAC = AC + BAC - EV$ to calculate EAC. So, EAC = 75,000+100,000-85,000 = 90,000.

B. In this instance with the information provided you are being lead to use $EAC = AC + BAC - EV$ to calculate EAC. So, EAC = 75,000+100,000-85,000 = 90,000.

C. In this instance with the information provided you are being lead to use $EAC = AC + BAC - EV$ to calculate EAC. So, EAC = 75,000+100,000-85,000 = 90,000.

D. In this instance with the information provided you are being lead to use $EAC = AC + BAC - EV$ to calculate EAC. So, EAC = 75,000+100,000-85,000 = 90,000.

190: The correct answer is C

A. This question requires you to first work out the CPI which is EV/AC = 40,000/45,000 = 0.88. Then use this number in the equation EAC= BAC/cumulative CPI = 50,000/.88 = 56,818.

B. This question requires you to first work out the CPI which is EV/AC = 40,000/45,000 = 0.88. Then use this number in the equation EAC= BAC/cumulative CPI = 50,000/.88 = 56,818.

C. This question requires you to first work out the CPI which is EV/AC = 40,000/45,000 = 0.88. Then use this number in the equation EAC= BAC/cumulative CPI = 50,000/.88 = 56,818.

D. This question requires you to first work out the CPI which is EV/AC = 40,000/45,000 = 0.88. Then use this number in the equation EAC= BAC/cumulative CPI = 50,000/.88 = 56,818.

191: The correct answer is B

A. The estimate to complete is the estimate of the amount of funds required to complete the project and is the difference between you EAC and AC.
B. The to-complete performance index (TCPI) is a useful tool for assessing the actual financial performance of the project baseline against actual performance and the amount of cost based work required to finish the project.
C. The cost baseline is the approved project budget.
D. Earned value is the value of work performed.

192: The correct answer is D

A. EAC using both SPI and CPI factors = AC + [(BAC-EV)/(cumulative CPI x cumulative SPI)] = 10,000 + [(20,000-8,000)/(0.8 x 0.9)] = 10,000 + [(12,000/.72)] = 26,666.
B. EAC using both SPI and CPI factors = AC + [(BAC-EV)/(cumulative CPI x cumulative SPI)] = 10,000 + [(20,000-8,000)/(0.8 x 0.9)] = 10,000 + [(12,000/.72)] = 26,666.
C. EAC using both SPI and CPI factors = AC + [(BAC-EV)/(cumulative CPI x cumulative SPI)] = 10,000 + [(20,000-8,000)/(0.8 x 0.9)] = 10,000 + [(12,000/.72)] = 26,666.
D. EAC using both SPI and CPI factors = AC + [(BAC-EV)/(cumulative CPI x cumulative SPI)] = 10,000 + [(20,000-8,000)/(0.8 x 0.9)] = 10,000 + [(12,000/.72)] = 26,666.

193: The correct answer is D

A. Change requests are an output from the Control Costs process.
B. Work performance information is an output from the Control Costs process.
C. Cost forecasts are an output from the Control Costs process.
D. Variance analysis is a tool that examines the difference between where you thought you should be in the project and where you actually are. It is used as a tool and technique in several of the monitoring and controlling processes.

194: The correct answer is A

A. *The current budget of the project contains all of the authorized funding for the project including additions to the project since the setting of the original baselines.*

B. *The current budget of the project contains all of the authorized funding for the project including additions to the project since the setting of the original baselines. This includes any and all authorized work done on the project, including the investigation of work that may be done to investigate the feasibility of changes.*

C. *The current budget of the project contains all of the authorized funding for the project including additions to the project since the setting of the original baselines.*

D. *The current budget of the project contains all of the authorized funding for the project including additions to the project since the setting of the original baselines.*

195: The correct answer is C

A. *In order to calculate the TCPI you need to use the formula (BAC-EV)/(BAC-AC) which gives an answer of 0.93.*

B. *In order to calculate the TCPI you need to use the formula (BAC-EV)/(BAC-AC) which gives an answer of 0.93. This answer would be calculated. If you got EV and AC around the wrong way.*

C. *In order to calculate the TCPI you need to use the formula (BAC-EV)/(BAC-AC) which gives an answer of 0.93.*

D. *In order to calculate the TCPI you need to use the formula (BAC-EV)/(BAC-AC) which gives an answer of 0.93.*

196: The correct answer is D

A. *This answer is incorrect because both continuous improvement, or Kaizen, and prevention over inspection are a fundamental concepts underlying quality management but they do not directly link to customer satisfaction.*

B. *This answer is incorrect because prevention over inspection is a fundamental concept underlying quality management but it does not directly link to customer satisfaction.*

C. *This answer is incorrect because continuous improvement, or Kaizen, is a fundamental concept underlying quality management but it does not directly link to customer satisfaction.*

D. The product's conformance to the customers requirements and the fitness of use of the product are both factors in achieving customer satisfaction and defining quality of product.

197: The correct answer is C

A. The correct answer is failure mode and effect analysis (FMEA) which is one of several non-proprietary approaches to quality management.
B. The correct answer is failure mode and effect analysis (FMEA) which is one of several non-proprietary approaches to quality management.
C. Failure mode and effect analysis (FMEA) is one of several non-proprietary approaches to quality management.
D. The correct answer is failure mode and effect analysis (FMEA) which is one of several non-proprietary approaches to quality management.

198: The correct answer is D

A. Customer satisfaction is one of four characteristics shared by quality management and project management.
B. Prevention over inspection is one of four characteristics shared by quality management and project management.
C. Continuous inspection is one of four characteristics shared by quality management and project management.
D. Total quality management is an approach to quality the other three answers are all characteristics shared by quality management and project management. The fourth characteristic is management responsibility.

199: The correct answer is D

A. This answer is incorrect because building in the quality systems to minimize the amount of defects found via inspection is generally cheaper in the long run that having to perform rework to fix defects found by inspection.
B. This answer is incorrect because building in the quality systems to minimize the amount of defects found via inspection is generally cheaper in the long run that having to perform rework to fix defects found by inspection.

C. This answer is incorrect because building in the quality systems to minimize the amount of defects found via inspection is generally cheaper in the long run that having to perform rework to fix defects found by inspection.

D. Building in the quality systems to minimize the amount of defects found via inspection is generally cheaper in the long run that having to perform rework to fix defects found by inspection.

200: The correct answer is B

A. This answer is incorrect because precision means the values of the repeated measurements are clustered and have little scatter. Accuracy means that the measured value is very close to the true value

B. This answer is correct and you need to know there is a difference between precision and accuracy and for the exam you need to know how and when to use the two terms.

C. This answer is incorrect because precision means the values of the repeated measurements are clustered and have little scatter. Accuracy means that the measured value is very close to the true value

D. This answer is incorrect because precision means the values of the repeated measurements are clustered and have little scatter. Accuracy means that the measured value is very close to the true value

201: The correct answer is C

A. Quality of the project relates to the degree to which the project is run according to the agreed project management plan. Quality of the product relates to the ability of the product to meet customer requirements.

B. Quality of the project relates to the degree to which the project is run according to the agreed project management plan. Quality of the product relates to the ability of the product to meet customer requirements.

C. Quality of the project relates to the degree to which the project is run according to the agreed project management plan. Quality of the product relates to the ability of the product to meet customer requirements.

D. Quality of the project relates to the degree to which the project is run according to the agreed project management plan. Quality of the product relates to the ability of the product to meet customer requirements.

202: The correct answer is C

A. *Quality on a project can be adversely affected in a number of ways. Overworking staff can cause human errors to creep in to the process and should be recognized within the quality management plan.*

B. *Quality on a project can be adversely affected in a number of ways. Overworking staff can cause human errors to creep in to the process and should be recognized within the quality management plan.*

C. *Quality on a project can be adversely affected in a number of ways. Overworking staff can cause human errors to creep in to the process and should be recognized within the quality management plan.*

D. *Quality on a project can be adversely affected in a number of ways. Overworking staff can cause human errors to creep in to the process and should be recognized within the quality management plan.*

203: The correct answer is B

A. *Did you read this question properly? There isn't any problem with this scenario so there is no need to act. Quality and grade are different. You can manufacture a high or low grade product depending on what the customer specifie,.*

B. *Quality and grade are different. You can manufacture a high or low grade product depending on what the customer specified, so finding a low grade product is probably exactly in line with the customer specifications.*

C. *Did you read this question properly? There isn't any problem with this scenario so there is no need to act. Quality and grade are different. You can manufacture a high or low grade product depending on what the customer specified, so finding a low grade p*

D. *Did you read this question properly? There isn't any problem with this scenario so there is no need to act. Quality and grade are different. You can manufacture a high or low grade product depending on what the customer specified, so finding a low grade product may be expected.*

204: The correct answer is B

A. *Kanban is not correct. It is a Japanese term for visual card based system for inventory or work control.*

B. *Kaizen means improvement in Japanese. It means continuing improvement involving everyone, including managers and workers alike, from the top to the bottom of the organization.*

C. *Kawasaki is not the correct term. Kawasaki is a Japanese manufacturer of motorized vehicles.*

D. Kampai is not correct. It is a Japanese term used when making a toast usually when drinking alcohol.

205: The correct answer is A

A. There are several important proprietary and non-proprietary quality management models that you should be aware of. The work by Shewhart and Deming produced the plan-do-check-act cycle for quality management.
B. The Organizational Project Management Maturity Model (OPM3) is a tool for measuring the level of project management maturity within an organization.
C. Six Sigma is a proprietary quality management tool focused on eliminating errors.
D. Total quality management is a quality system that holds all parties involved in quality management accountable for ensuring quality.

206: The correct answer is B

A. The cost of quality refers to the whole of the product life cycle which includes not only the cost of quality during manufacture but also the cost of product returns, warranty claims, and recall campaigns over the life of the product.
B. The cost of quality refers to the whole of the product life cycle which includes not only the cost of quality during manufacture but also the cost of product returns, warranty claims, and recall campaigns over the life of the product.
C. The cost of quality refers to the whole of the product life cycle which includes not only the cost of quality during manufacture but also the cost of product returns, warranty claims, and recall campaigns over the life of the product.
D. The cost of quality refers to the whole of the product life cycle which includes not only the cost of quality during manufacture but also the cost of product returns, warranty claims, and recall campaigns over the life of the product.

207: The correct answer is D

A. Perform Quality Assurance is the process of auditing quality requirements and processes.

B. The cost of quality refers to the whole of the product life cycle which includes not only the cost of quality during manufacture but also the cost of product returns, warranty claims, and recall campaigns over the life of the product.

C. Control Quality is the process of monitoring and recording results of executing quality activities.

D. Plan Quality Management is the process of identifying quality requirements and standards for both the project and product.

208: The correct answer is B

A. The stakeholder register is one of the inputs into the Plan Quality Management process.

B. Quality checklists are an output from the Plan Quality Management process.

C. The risk register is one of the inputs into the Plan Quality Management process.

D. The requirements documentation is one of the inputs into the Plan Quality Management process.

209: The correct answer is A

A. Destructive testing loss is a specific cost of conformance not a general characteristic of cost of quality.

B. Cost of quality does include investment in preventing non-conformance to requirements.

C. Cost of quality does include appraising the product or service for conformance to requirements

D. Cost of quality does include consideration of the impact of failing to meet requirements

210: The correct answer is A

A. Rework is a cost of non-conformance in that it is incurred when you do not conform with the quality plan;

B. Equipment is part of prevention costs of conformance to build a quality product.

C. Training is part of prevention costs of conformance to build a quality product.

D. Equipment is part of appraisal costs of conformance to assess the quality.

211: The correct answer is D

A. A control chart measures and tracks quality data and assesses it within predetermined upper and lower control limits.
B. A control chart measures and tracks quality data and assesses it within predetermined upper and lower control limits.
C. A control chart measures and tracks quality data and assesses it within predetermined upper and lower control limits.
D. A control chart measures and tracks quality data and assesses it within predetermined upper and lower control limits.

212: The correct answer is A

A. The third result is outside of the control limits and should be investigated.
B. You should not just continue working as the third result is outside of the control limits and should be investigated.
C. The question does not give you the tenth result.
D. The first result is within the control limits so does not need investigating.

213: The correct answer is C

A. This is an example of the rule of 7 where there are 7 or more consecutive points either above or below the mean which indicates the process is moving out of acceptable limits so the team needs to investigate and determine the assignable cause.
B. You should not simply change the control limits. This scenario indicates the rule of 7 and requires investigation and for you to find the cause.
C. This is an example of the rule of 7 where there are 7 or more consecutive points either above or below the mean which indicates the process is moving out of acceptable limits so the team needs to investigate and determine the assignable cause.
D. Firing the quality assurance team will not solve the problem. This scenario indicates the rule of 7 and requires investigation and for you to find the cause.

214: The correct answer is C

A. Control limits are generally set at 3 standard deviations above and below the acceptable mean of data.
B. Control limits are generally set at 3 standard deviations above and below the acceptable mean of data.
C. Control limits are generally set at 3 standard deviations above and below the acceptable mean of data.
D. Control limits are generally set at 3 standard deviations above and below the acceptable mean of data.

215: The correct answer is A

A. Data outside the upper or lower control limits, or seven consecutive points above or below the mean indicate the process is out of control and requires corrective action.
B. This is an example of the rule of 7 where there are 7 or more consecutive points either above or below the mean which indicates the process is moving out of acceptable limits so the team needs to investigate and determine the assignable cause.
C. This is a good option but not the best option. You should first refer to your quality management plan which may direct you to stop work immediately and investigate the root cause of the problem.
D. You should not simply change the control limits. This scenario indicates the rule of 7 and requires investigation and for you to find the cause.

216: The correct answer is C

A. This is a good option but not the best option. You should first refer to your quality management plan which may direct you to stop work immediately and investigate the root cause of the problem.
B. You should not do nothing as data that is beneath the lower control limit but above the lower specification limit indicates that product is still within the customer specification but may be in need of corrective action to ensure it stays there.
C. Data that is beneath the lower control limit but above the lower specification limit indicates that product is still within the customer specification but may be in need of corrective action to ensure it stays there.

D. You should not simply change the control limits. Data that is beneath the lower control limit but above the lower specification limit indicates that product is still within the customer specification but may be in need of corrective action to ensure it stays within the limits

217: The correct answer is A

A. Design of experiments is a statistical method for identifying which factors may influence specific variables or a product or a process under development.
B. Analogous estimating is used for estimating time or cost
C. Benchmarking is the technique of comparing your quality activities to another project or organization.
D. Cost of quality considers the cost of quality decision you make over the life of the product.

218: The correct answer is B

A. Analogous estimating is used for estimating time or cost
B. Benchmarking is a process of comparing your projects to others in relation to quality management.
C. Design of experiments is a statistical method for identifying which factors may influence specific variables or a product or a process under development.
D. Cost of quality considers the cost of quality decision you make over the life of the product.

219: The correct answer is C

A. Inspection is physically inspecting a product for defects.
B. Flowcharting is a technique for graphically mapping a quality process.
C. It is less expensive to examine only a part of the population.
D. This answer is incorrect because it is not a term referenced within the PMBOK® Guide.

220: The correct answer is D

A. This answer is incorrect because it is a made up quality term.

B. Design of experiments is a statistical method for identifying which factors may influence specific variables or a product or a process under development.

C. Benchmarking is the technique of comparing your quality activities to another project or organization.

D. When you have a large amount of data to check it can be too time consuming and cost too much to examine every product. In this case just taking a relevant sample and extrapolating the quality of this sample to the whole data range is much more efficient.

221: The correct answer is D

A. An affinity diagram is a quality management tool and provides a graphical method of structuring and displaying a large number of discrete pieces of information

B. A force field diagram is a quality planning tool that is used to weigh up the points for and against a potential decision or action.

C. Matrix diagrams are a quality management tool and are used to compare information between two or more lists.

D. Quality checklists are an output, not a tool, from the Plan Quality Management process.

222: The correct answer is D

A. Failure rate is a quality metric that records the number of failures and there impact.

B. Budget control is a quality metric used to align quality decisions with the project budget.

C. Defect frequency is a quality metric that measures the frequency of defects discovered and is used for root cause analysis.

D. The upper control limit is part of the control chart tool and it is not a quality metric.

223: The correct answer is D

A. The quality management plan is the primary output from the Plan Quality Management process.

B. Quality metrics are an output from the Plan Quality Management process and are used throughout the other quality processes.

C. The process improvement plan is an output from the Plan Quality Management process.
D. Flowcharting is not an output, it is a technique used in the Plan Quality Management process.

224: The correct answer is A

A. Perform quality assurance is an executing process that is focused on constantly improving the quality processes on the project.
B. Plan Quality Management is a process which produces the quality management plan.
C. Control Quality is the process of monitoring and recording results of executing quality activities.
D. Progressive elaboration is a form of iterative planning.

225: The correct answer is A

A. Quality audits are a technique used in the Perform Quality Assurance process, not an input.
B. The process improvement plan is an important input into the Perform Quality Assurance process as it outlines how processes will be improved.
C. Quality metrics are an input into the Perform Quality Assurance process as they guide the assessment of quality assurance activities.
D. Quality control measurements are an input into the Perform Quality Assurance process as the are used to determine if processes are being performed as planned.

226: The correct answer is B

A. The quality audit focuses upon the quality processes of the project and is not generally focused upon the quality of the product of the project.
B. The quality audit focuses upon the quality processes of the project and is not generally focused upon the quality of the product of the project.
C. The quality audit focuses upon the quality processes of the project and is not generally focused upon the quality of the product of the project.
D. The quality audit focuses upon the quality processes of the project and is not generally focused upon the quality of the product of the project.

227: The correct answer is B

A. Quality metrics are an input into the Perform Quality Assurance process as they guide the assessment of quality assurance activities.
B. Change requests are an important output from the Perform Quality Assurance process as a result of your constant examination of the quality processes and procedures of your project.
C. Quality audits are a technique used in the Perform Quality Assurance process, not an output
D. Process analysis is a technique used in the Perform Quality Assurance process, not an output

228: The correct answer is B

A. The Perform Quality Assurance process examines the process of the project.
B. Control Quality is part of the monitoring and control process group.
C. The Plan Quality Management process produces the quality management plan.
D. Statistical sampling is a tool for taking a small sample from a large population and extrapolating results of the sample to the entire population.

229: The correct answer is C

A. Prevention and inspection are two different concepts in the quality management area. Prevention is designed to keep errors out of the process while inspection is about discovering the errors prior to handover.
B. Prevention and inspection are two different concepts in the quality management area. Prevention is designed to keep errors out of the process while inspection is about discovering the errors prior to handover.
C. Prevention and inspection are two different concepts in the quality management area. Prevention is designed to keep errors out of the process while inspection is about discovering the errors prior to handover.
D. Prevention and inspection are two different concepts in the quality management area. Prevention is designed to keep errors out of the process while inspection is about discovering the errors prior to handover.

230: The correct answer is D

A. This answer is incorrect because tolerances specify the acceptable range of specifications while control limits indicate that a process may be out of control.

B. *This answer is incorrect because tolerances specify the acceptable range of specifications while control limits indicate that a process may be out of control.*

C. *This answer is incorrect because tolerances specify the acceptable range of specifications while control limits indicate that a process may be out of control.*

D. *Tolerances specify the acceptable range of specifications while control limits indicate that a process may be out of control.*

231: The correct answer is D

A. *The 7 tools of quality according to Ishikawa are: Cause and Effect diagrams, Control Charts, Flowcharting, Histograms, Pareto charts, Run Charts, and Scatter Diagrams.*

B. *The 7 tools of quality according to Ishikawa are: Cause and Effect diagrams, Control Charts, Flowcharting, Histograms, Pareto charts, Run Charts, and Scatter Diagrams.*

C. *The 7 tools of quality according to Ishikawa are: Cause and Effect diagrams, Control Charts, Flowcharting, Histograms, Pareto charts, Run Charts, and Scatter Diagrams.*

D. *Inspection is not one of Ishikawa's seven tools of quality. The 7 tools of quality according to Ishikawa are: Cause and Effect diagrams, Control Charts, Flowcharting, Histograms, Pareto charts, Run Charts, and Scatter Diagrams.*

232: The correct answer is D

A. *A scatter diagram plots the results of two variables on an x and y axis diagram.*

B. *This answer is not correct because it is not a term referenced within the PMBOK® Guide.*

C. *A Pareto diagram or chart determines frequency of defects and arranges them in hierarchical order so you can determine which defects are causing the most problems, this is often called the 80:20 rule.*

D. *The diagram is a cause and effect diagram, also known as a fishbone or Ishikawa diagram as well.*

233: The correct answer is B

A. Control charts identify when a process may be going out of control, they do not help find the cause of the problem.

B. A cause and effect diagram, also known as an Ishikawa or fishbone (on account of its shape) tries to determine the root cause of a problem so the cause and not the symptom is identified.

C. A Pareto diagram or chart determines frequency of defects and arranges them in hierarchical order so you can determine which defects are causing the most problems, this is often called the 80:20 rule.

D. A run chart plots a particular variable over a period of time.

234: The correct answer is D

A. This answer is not correct because it is not a term referenced within the PMBOK® Guide.

B. This answer is not correct because it is a combination of two familiar words that when put together are a made up term.

C. A cause and effect diagram, also known as an Ishikawa or fishbone (on account of its shape) tries to determine the root cause of a problem so the cause and not the symptom is identified.

D. A Pareto diagram is a histogram, ordered by frequency of occurrence, that shows how many results were generated by type or category of identified cause. By using this tool the manager can identify the defects that occurred most often.

235: The correct answer is B

A. A scatter diagram plots the results of two variables on an x and y axis diagram.

B. A pareto chart is a type of histogram that shows the rank ordering of defects by type of category so that corrective action can be focused in the correct place.

C. Control charts identify when a process may be going out of control, they do not help find the cause of the problem.

D. A histogram, or bar chart, can be used for graphically representing the frequency of events.

236: The correct answer is D

A. A scatter diagram plots the results of two variables on an x and y axis diagram.

B. A Pareto diagram is a histogram, ordered by frequency of occurrence, that shows how many results were generated by type or category of identified cause. However, in this question you should see a Pareto chart as a subset of histograms which is the best answer.

C. Control charts identify when a process may be going out of control, they do not help find the cause of the problem.

D. A histogram or bar chart is one of the most commonly used and easiest to understand visual representations of information, especially to show relationships between different areas.

237: The correct answer is B

A. Control charts identify when a process may be going out of control, they do not help find the cause of the problem.

B. A run chart is a simplified control chart without the displayed limits that can indicate a trend over time, and forecast future outcomes based on historical results using such techniques as linear regression.

C. A Pareto diagram is a histogram, ordered by frequency of occurrence, that shows how many results were generated by type or category of identified cause. By using this tool the manager can identify the defects that occurred most often.

D. A cause and effect diagram, also known as an Ishikawa or fishbone (on account of its shape) tries to determine the root cause of a problem so the cause and not the symptom is identified.

238: The correct answer is B

A. A Pareto diagram is a histogram, ordered by frequency of occurrence, that shows how many results were generated by type or category of identified cause. By using this tool the manager can identify the defects that occurred most often.

B. A scatter diagram plots the relationship between 2 variables, 1 on the x axis and 1 on the y axis.

C. Control charts identify when a process may be going out of control, they do not help find the cause of the problem.

D. A run chart is a simplified control chart without the displayed limits that can indicate a trend over time, and forecast future outcomes based on historical results using such techniques as linear regression.

239: The correct answer is B

A. Validated changes are an output as they are work required by an approved change request that has been checked for quality.
B. Quality metrics is an input into the Control Quality process.
C. As a result of carrying out this monitoring and controlling process it may be necessary to generate change requests as an output as a result of variances discovered.
D. Quality control measurements are the primary output from the Control Quality process.

240: The correct answer is D

A. This may seem like a sensible answer but team building and development is only one part of project human resource management which is the best answer.
B. This may seem like a sensible answer but managing the project team is only one part of project human resource management which is the best answer.
C. Project management covers the entire profession and all the knowledge areas. Project human resource management is the specific area that organizes, recruits, rewards, manages and leads the project team
D. This is the correct collective term for all of the processes that make up the human resource management knowledge area.

241: The correct answer is D

A. The project sponsor is responsible for securing financial support and funding for the project.
B. The project sponsor has the responsibility for influencing high level stakeholders to provide political and financial support for the project.
C. The project sponsor has the responsibility for monitoring the progress of the project at a high level. They are not responsible for low level monitoring, that is the responsibility of the project manager.
D. The project sponsor performs a high level role and is responsible for ensuring the project has the funding it requires, monitoring progress, acting as project champion and influencing others in support of the project.

242: The correct answer is D

A. This answer is incorrect because the process generally follows the sequence of first plan, then do what you planned, then check that what you are doing is correct.

B. This answer is incorrect because the process generally follows the sequence of first plan, then do what you planned, then check that what you are doing is correct. So first plan your approach to getting, developing and managing your human resources. Next, using the plan, you acquire your project team, then develop them, and finally monitor or manage them.

C. This answer is incorrect because the process generally follows the sequence of first plan, then do what you planned, then check that what you are doing is correct.

D. This process generally follows the sequence of first plan, then do what you planned, then check that what you are doing is correct.

243: The correct answer is C

A. The Identify Risks process uses information from the human resource management plan to identify risks associated with human resources.

B. The Estimate Costs process using the human resource management plan to assist in estimating costs associated with human resources on the project.

C. The outputs from the Estimate Activity Resources process are used as inputs into the Plan Human Resource Management process.

D. The Acquire Project Team process uses the human resource management plan to recruit the team members.

244: The correct answer is C

A. Enterprise environmental factors such as external market conditions for salaries and employment law are an input into the Plan Human Resource Management process.

B. You need the activity resource requirements to know what work you need people to complete and how much work is needed to be done.

C. You don't need the WBS to prepare your human resource management plan but any changes to the WBS may mean changes to your HR plan.

D. Organizational process assets such as existing recruitment policies are an input into the Plan Human Resource Management process.

245: The correct answer is A

A. *The organizational breakdown structure is arranged according to an organizations existing departments, units, or teams with the project activities or work packages listed under each department.*
B. *The work breakdown structure (WBS) does not show any information about the organizational structure, it decomposes deliverables down into work packages.*
C. *The resource breakdown structure (RBS) does not show any information about the organizational structure, it breaks down the resources required for the project.*
D. *The responsibility assignment matrix (RAM) does not show any information about the organizational structure, it shows people who is responsibility for individual work packages and activities.*

246: The correct answer is B

A. *The organizational breakdown structure is arranged according to an organizations existing departments, units, or teams with the project activities or work packages listed under each department. It does not show who is responsible, accountable, consulted,*
B. *A RACI chart is a specific type of responsibility assignment matrix (RAM) that lists additional information about the responsibilities, accountable , who is to be consulted and who is to be informed in relation to project activities.*
C. *The work breakdown structure (WBS) does not show any information who is responsible, accountable, consulted, and informed about the work, it decomposes deliverables down into work packages.*
D. *A RACI chart is a specific type of responsibility assignment matrix (RAM) and as such it is the best answer.*

247: The correct answer is D

A. *Herzberg's motivation-hygiene theory says that employees requires hygiene factors to be present before motivation factors will work.*
B. *Maslow's hierarchy needs specifies a set of needs an individual will seek to fulfill with the current need being the strongest motivator.*
C. *McGregor's theory X and theory Y summarizes management views of employees as either naturally unmotivated and untrustworthy (theory X) or naturally motivated and trustworthy (Theory Y)*
D. *This answer is not correct because it is not a term referenced within the PMBOK® Guide.*

248: The correct answer is C

A. Vrooms expectancy theory states that the expectation of receiving a reward for a certain accomplishment will motivate people to work harder but this will only work if the accomplishment is perceived to be achievable

B. Ouchi's theory Z says that organizations should seek to fulfill a large role in an employees life beyond just an employment agreement.
C. This answer is not correct because it is not a term referenced within the PMBOK® Guide.
D. McClelland's Human Motivation, Achievement or Three Needs Theory states that people are motivated to work by the need for achievement, power and affiliation.

249: The correct answer is C

A. The human resource management plan may have project organization charts to team members can see reporting lines and relationships within the organization.
B. The human resource management plan will include the staffing management plan which specifies how and when project team members will be required on the project.
C. Costs estimates for staff time will be included in your cost management plan.
D. The human resource management plan will have a description of team members roles and responsibilities.

250: The correct answer is A

A. The resource calendar will clearly show what resources you need, when you need them and how much commitment they need to have when you need them as well as any constraints upon the time they can give to the project such as other work commitments, working
B. The resource calendar does not show the cost of staff members over time. This will be in your project cost baseline. The resource calendar will clearly show what resources you need, when you need them and how much commitment they need to have when you need them as well as any constraints upon the time they can give to the project such as other work commitments, working hours and holidays.

C. Annual leave may be a small part of the resource calendar but it is not the best answer to this questions. The resource calendar will clearly show what resources you need, when you need them and how much commitment they need to have when you need them as

D. Programmed team building activities throughout the project will not be shown on the resource calendar. The resource calendar will clearly show what resources you need, when you need them and how much commitment they need to have when you need them as well

251: The correct answer is B

A. Decreased customer satisfaction is a very real potential outcome as the work may not start on time nor be produced to the expected quality.

B. It is very doubtful that failure to acquire your project team would result in reduced project costs as there will most likely be delays associated with getting alternate team members.

C. Recued quality is a potential adverse effects caused by delays and also less experienced people working on the project.

D. Failing to acquire the staff you need when you need them will result in delays to the project schedule.

252: The correct answer is A

A. You have a responsibility, where possible, to provide training for your team members to ensure they have the appropriate skills to complete the work asked of them.

B. Firing the team member would not solve the problem which is a lack of training

C. Learning on the job is not the safest or most efficient way to get team members trained

D. Assigning the team member to another project does not deal with the real issue which is a lack of training.

253: The correct answer is A

A. This is an example of a negotiation within a matrix organization for human resource.

B. Pre-assignment of staff does not involve negotiations such as outlined in the question.

C. Acquisition is the procedure of searching outside the organization for team members.

D. Acquire Project Team is the process that includes negotiation, which is the best answer to this question.

254: The correct answer is B

A. This will only cause problems in the long term as 10am your time may be 3am for someone else. Use of virtual teams is increasingly common and provides many potential benefits. There are additional risks associated with managing team members who you may ne

B. Use of virtual teams is increasingly common and provides many potential benefits. There are additional risks associated with managing team members who you may never meet face to face but the use of electronic video conferencing is a great way to overcome some of the communication problems.

C. Running multiple meetings on the same topic is not an efficient way to deal with this issue. Use of virtual teams is increasingly common and provides many potential benefits. There are additional risks associated with managing team members who you may nev

D. Acquire Project Team is the process that includes negotiation, which is the best answer to this question.

255: The correct answer is A

A. Develop Project Team is the executing process of making sure your team is capable of performing the work expected of it.

B. Plan Human Resource Management is the process of producing the human resource management plan.

C. Acquire Project Team is the process of obtaining your project team members as outlined in your human resource management plan.

D. Manage Project Team is the process of ensuring your team are performing optimally and improving the performance of the team.

256: The correct answer is A

A. There are several methods for resolving conflict: forcing, withdrawal, smoothing, compromise, and problem solving. Of these, problem solving is the best

B. This answer proposes withdrawing from addressing the conflict. There are several methods for resolving conflict: forcing, withdrawal, smoothing, compromise, and problem solving. Of these, problem solving is the best, because the new facts allow the two disagreeing parties to resolve their differences with factual information and not opinion.

C. This answer suggest forcing as a method to resolve the conflict. There are several methods for resolving conflict: forcing, withdrawal, smoothing, compromise, and problem solving.

D. Compromise does not deal with the root cause of the problem. There are several methods for resolving conflict: forcing, withdrawal, smoothing, compromise, and problem solving. Of these, problem solving is the best.

257: The correct answer is A

A. As project manager you must recognize that when working on a project with people from different cultures that it is important to recognize these and not try to assimilate everyone to one particular culture.

B. Improving team members knowledge and skills is a key objective of the Develop Project Team process.

C. Improving trust and agreement between team members is a key objective of the Develop Project Team process.

D. Creating a dynamic and cohesive team culture is a key objective of the Develop Project Team process.

258: The correct answer is D

A. The Tuckman 5 stage model of team development outlines the stages a group of people will go through. A team will first go through the forming stage, then storming, then norming, before reaching the performing stage, and finally adjourning.

B. The Tuckman 5 stage model of team development outlines the stages a group of people will go through. A team will first go through the forming stage, then storming, then norming, before reaching the performing stage, and finally adjourning. A team can also drop back several stages in the model when an existing team member leaves or a new team members joins.

C. The Tuckman 5 stage model of team development outlines the stages a group of people will go through. A team will first go through the forming stage, then storming, then norming, before reaching the performing stage, and finally adjourning.

D. The Tuckman 5 stage model of team development outlines the stages a group of people will go through. A team will first go through the forming stage, then storming, then norming, before reaching the performing stage, and finally adjourning.

259: The correct answer is B

A. The amount of money offered is probably not the problem as you will find that other motivations such as power, achievement and affiliation are better.

B. Deciding the appropriate recognition and rewards requires the project manager to know exactly what motivates people. People generally only want rewards that they value and recent research has shown that money is not generally the highest motivator for people. Praise and opportunity for advancement is often more highly sought after.

C. The amount of money offered is probably not the problem as you will find that other motivations such as power, achievement and affiliation are better.

D. Whether or not your project team respect you as a project manager it is more likely that this scenario is because your team culture does not support individualism.

260: The correct answer is C

A. Assignment generally refers to assigning team members to specific roles and responsibilities.

B. This answer is incorrect because it is not a term referenced within the PMBOK® Guide.

C. Co-locating team members where possible improves team performance.

D. A war room is a specific meeting room for project team members to be collocated and focus on doing the project work. The best answer to this question is co-location.

261: The correct answer is B

A. Team building activities may sound like the correct answer but they are a tool or technique used during the Develop Project Team process.

B. The Develop Project Team process is focused on ensuring the team has the necessary skills to complete the work required of them. To ensure this is effectively done you need to have team performance assessments.

C. *Project staff assignments are an output from the Acquire Project Team process.*
D. *WBS dictionary elements are part of the WBS dictionary which is created during the Create WBS process.*

262: The correct answer is C

A. *Team management involves combination of skills with special emphasis on communication, conflict management, negotiation, and leadership.*
B. *Team management involves combination of skills with special emphasis on communication, conflict management, negotiation, and leadership.*
C. *Effective management of your project team is critical to the success of the project. Team management involves combination of skills with special emphasis on communication, conflict management, negotiation, and leadership.*
D. *Team management involves combination of skills with special emphasis on communication, conflict management, negotiation, and leadership.*

263: The correct answer is C

A. *Project management plan as an input into the Manage Project Team process*
B. *Project staff assignments are an input into the Manage Project Team process*
C. *Project performance appraisals are a tool or technique used in the Manage Project Team process.*
D. *Team performance assessments are a useful input into the Manage Project Team process as they get information about how well the team is performing*

264: The correct answer is B

A. *Work satisfaction and fringe benefits are classified as satisfied as in Hertzberg's theory of motivation*
B. *This is an example of a questions that the PMBOK® Guide does not have the answer for. It requires you to have additional knowledge about the leading theories are managing people.*
C. *Plush office space and performance-based salary raises are classified as satisfied as in Hertzberg's theory of motivation*

D. Vacation time, assignment of personal staff assistant are factors that are classified as satisfied as in Hertzberg's theory of motivation

265: The correct answer is D

A. A project manager must have effective decision-making skills as part of the suite of interpersonal skills that they have.
B. Having the ability to persuade people, and having mature listening skills are key interpersonal skills for a project manager to have.
C. Strong and well developed leadership skills that can operate in a variety of scenarios are an essential interpersonal skill for a project manager.
D. A focus on prevention over inspection and an eye for detail when reporting your project status reports is a strong technical, not interpersonal skill.

266: The correct answer is B

A. Forcing a solution upon participants and of conflict is not a long-lasting and conflict will eventually resurface
B. Confronting or problem and looking for a clear and permanent solution is the best way to resolve conflict. Your own personal conflict resolution style and any that you choose to adopt will dictate how successful you are in resolving conflict. Remember that conflict is not necessarily a bad thing but can lead to poor performance if not managed well.
C. Smoothing over a conflict situation in the hope that it will go away will not result in a permanent solution to the conflict
D. Withdrawing from, and avoiding dealing with conflict does not deal with the issue in a proactive manner and eventually the conflict will have adverse effects upon team performance and ultimately the chances of project success.

267: The correct answer is C

A. Vision and humor are important elements of effective leadership but not as important as respect and trust. Leadership is an important facet of the interpersonal skills you must be aware of and develop throughout your career as a project manager.

B. Friendship and admiration may arise from your effective leadership, but they are based on the key elements of respect and trust. Leadership is an important facet of the interpersonal skills you must be aware of and develop throughout your career as a project manager. Central to effective leadership are the soft skills including the ability to generate respect and trust for yourself from your team members, and also to give respect and trust to your team members.

C. Leadership is an important facet of the interpersonal skills you must be aware of and develop throughout your career as a project manager. Central to effective leadership are the soft skills including the ability to generate respect and trust for yourself

D. Fear and submission are not good elements of effective leadership. Leadership is an important facet of the interpersonal skills you must be aware of and develop throughout your career as a project manager.

268: The correct answer is C

A. The four basic decision styles are command, consultation, consensus, and coin flip or random.

B. The four basic decision styles are command, consultation, consensus, and coin flip or random.

C. Ideas to action is not one of the four basic decision styles normally used by project managers. The four basic decision styles are command, consultation, consensus, and coin flip or random.

D. The four basic decision styles are command, consultation, consensus, and coin flip or random.

269: The correct answer is A

A. The 6-phase model is outlined in Appendix X3 on interpersonal skills of the PMBOK® Guide as an important interpersonal skill for managing your team.

B. Shewhart and Deming's Plan-Do-Check-Act cycle is the basis of modern project management and modern quality management. It is not used to make decisions.

C. Kouzes and Posner are names is generally associated with leadership development not decision-making and this answer is not a term referenced within the PMBOK® Guide.

D. This answer is incorrect because it is made up term.

270: The correct answer is C

A. In order to persuade a person or organisation formed an action, you will need to display very strong and well developed communication skills.
B. Setting in managing the expectations of stakeholders is achieved through the effective use of communication skills.
C. Reviewing the work breakdown structure is a technical, not a communication skill. We can not stress enough the role that effective communications plays in project success. Many people seem to think it is the technical financial, risk, quality, and scope m
D. Communication is a two-way process and therefore listening actively and effectively as a key communication skill.

271: The correct answer is B

A. Informal written forms of communication are best used for memos and internal notes. When dealing with changes to a contract, formal written forms of communication are best.
B. A contract is a legally binding document and as such all communication about contracts should be formal and in writing.
C. Formal verbal forms of communication are presentations and speeches. When dealing with changes to a contract, formal written forms of communication are best.
D. Electronic forms of communication include e-mails and Internet. When dealing with changes to a contract, formal written forms of communication are best.

272: The correct answer is B

A. Did you get this one wrong because you forgot to count yourself as well. There are 7 stakeholders and you as the project manager so that is 8 people, therefore the calculation is 8(8-1)/2 = 56/2 = 28.
B. Did you get this one wrong because you forgot to count yourself as well. There are 7 stakeholders and you as the project manager so that is 8 people, therefore the calculation is 8(8-1)/2 = 56/2 = 28.
C. Did you get this one wrong because you forgot to count yourself as well. There are 7 stakeholders and you as the project manager so that is 8 people, therefore the calculation is 8(8-1)/2 = 56/2 = 28.

D. *Did you get this one wrong because you forgot to count yourself as well. There are 7 stakeholders and you as the project manager so that is 8 people, therefore the calculation is 8(8-1)/2 = 56/2 = 28.*

273: The correct answer is C

A. *The question makes it clear that including you there are 12 stakeholders so the formula is 12(12-1)/2 = 132/2 = 66.*
B. *The question makes it clear that including you there are 12 stakeholders so the formula is 12(12-1)/2 = 132/2 = 66.*
C. *The question makes it clear that including you there are 12 stakeholders so the formula is 12(12-1)/2 = 132/2 = 66.*
D. *The question makes it clear that including you there are 12 stakeholders so the formula is 12(12-1)/2 = 132/2 = 66.*

274: The correct answer is C

A. *The type and availability of technology will influence the method of communications on your project. You must always select an appropriate method of communication to ensure it is effective.*
B. *The Duration o the project will effects on what style of communication you choose as you will have to keep stakeholders effectively engaged over longer periods od time. You must always select an appropriate method of communication to ensure it is effective.*
C. *Local government regulations are related to building and town planning matters and may effect your project in other ways but will not effect the communication distribution method.*
D. *The urgency of the information will influence the choice of communication method. You must always select an appropriate method of communication to ensure it is effective.*

275: The correct answer is D

A. *Cultural differences represent noise because there are many misunderstanding that arise because of different cultural expectations around appropriate forms of communication.*
B. *If one party is motivated to be part of the conversation occurring and one isn't then there will be a disruption to the communication.*
C. *Education differences can present problems in communication particular in the languages and medium chosen to communicate.*

D. Communication involves at least two people who may have very different backgrounds, experience, and education. Many times these individuals come from different cultures, speak different languages, and certainly have different drivers.

276: The correct answer is B

A. The asking somebody to write down the message won't improve your ability to understand. The solution to this problem is actively engage in effective listening.
B. Part of effective communication is ensuring that the message from sender to receiver is decoded properly. An effective way to do this is to repeat the key points back to get clarity.
C. It is your responsibility to ensure that you are actively engaged in effective listening to a conversation and postponing the meeting will only complicate communication matters.
D. The problem is not the speed at which the speaking, the problem is your ability to concentrate. To help you concentrate you could simply repeat the message back to the stakeholder.

277: The correct answer is C

A. By asking your project team to use English as a standardized language you are not trying to minimize environmental constraints you are trying to minimize noise and communications.
B. You are trying to minimize noise that may and corrupt communications not minimize cold references.
C. Noise is the term used to describe anything that gets in the way of the message between sender and receiver. Using English as a common language is an attempt to avoid the noise of different languages.
D. Simply by asking your team to use English as a first language does not minimize the use of foreign accents.

278: The correct answer is D

A. Simply agreeing with the speaker no good reason is not a sign of a good listener.
B. Taking good notes is an example of a good note taker not a good listener.
C. Finishing the speakers sentences is often considered quite rude and not the sign of a good listener.

D. Good listening is an important skill for any manager. One of the ways that you can become a skilled listener is by repeating some of the things that are said. Summarizing gives yourself and others a repeat of important points and makes the speaker feel mo

279: The correct answer is D

A. The stakeholder management strategy may guide some of your communications, particularly those in relation to stakeholder expectation management but they are not a type of communication method.
B. Pull communication occurs when the recipient must go to the source to get the communication
C. Interactive communication occurs when both sender and recipient engage in mutual exchange of information concurrently.
D. In this instance you are pushing the information out to stakeholders. Push communication occurs when the sender pushes the information to the recipient.

280: The correct answer is D

A. Encoding and decoding is what senders and receivers do in the standard communications model.
B. Push communication occurs when the sender pushes the information to the recipient.
C. Interactive communication occurs when both sender and recipient engage in mutual exchange of information concurrently.
D. It is called pull communication because recipients pull it down at their leisure rather than having it pushed to them.

281: The correct answer is C

A. This issue does not need to be escalated to the project sponsor as it is the responsibility of the project manager to make this decision.
B. The project team should not be left make this decision, it is the responsibility of the project manager to take responsibility.
C. It is the responsibility of the project manager to decide what, how, and when communication methods are to be used in the project.
D. The responsibility does not lie with any representative of a stakeholder is that could refer to anybody at all. The responsibility lies with the project manager.

282: The correct answer is D

A. At the core of the communication management plan will be stakeholder communication requirements.
B. The communications management plan will refer to the person who has responsibility for authorizing release of confidential information to stakeholders.
C. For ease of use and standardization, it is common for Communications management plan to have a glossary of common terminology.
D. You wouldn't normally find information as specific as team member addresses and phone numbers in the communications management plan.

283: The correct answer is B

A. Establishing ground rules for attendance conduct and follow-up at a meeting will make them more productive.
B. Meetings need to have structure around them and setting an agenda, ground rules and a set time for the meeting to run are good ways of improving efficiency. Teleconferencing is not a standardized way to make me more productive as the preference would be participants to be face-to-face.
C. Setting a clear start and finish times the meeting so that participants know when they should be there and when they will be would return to work is a way to make meetings more productive.
D. A clear and defined agenda which is followed will make meetings more efficient and productive.

284: The correct answer is C

A. Selecting the appropriate writing style to match the stakeholder needs is an effective information distribution technique
B. Presentation techniques are a very effective way of distributing information to stakeholders.
C. The issue log can be used as a communications tool to let stakeholders know these are being monitored but it is not a means of information distribution itself.
D. Selecting the correct an appropriate choice of media is an effective information distribution technique.

285: The correct answer is B

A. Manage Communications is part of the Executing process group.
B. Manage Communications is part of the Executing process group.
C. Manage Communications is part of the Executing process group.
D. Manage Communications is part of the Executing process group.

286: The correct answer is C

A. Humans are complex communicators and the non-verbal communications we make are always very important, often more so than the verbal communications we make.
B. Humans are complex communicators and the non-verbal communications we make are always very important, often more so than the verbal communications we make.
C. Humans are complex communicators and the non-verbal communications we make are always very important, often more so than the verbal communications we make.
D. Humans are complex communicators and the non-verbal communications we make are always very important, often more so than the verbal communications we make.

287: The correct answer is B

A. Using formal verbal, or any verbal form of communication could mean that the message was understood and forgotten. So in this instance a formal written form of communication is best.
B. As this situation is a serious one that needs to be documented for future reference you would be best to use formal written forms of communication.
C. As this situation is a serious one that needs to be documented for future reference you would be best to use formal, rather than informal, written forms of communication.
D. Using informal verbal, or any verbal form of communication could mean that the message was understood and forgotten. So in this instance a formal written form of communication is best.

288: The correct answer is A

A. This question requires you to take the normal formula for calculating communications channels and use it backwards. The formula is $(n(n-1))/2$. So working backwards we can see that the formula will be the answer is $((36\ x2)/9)+1 = 9$.

B. This question requires you to take the normal formula for calculating communications channels and use it backwards. The formula is $(n(n-1))/2$. So working backwards we can see that the formula will be the answer is $((36\ x2)/9)+1 = 9$

C. This question requires you to take the normal formula for calculating communications channels and use it backwards. The formula is $(n(n-1))/2$. So working backwards we can see that the formula will be the answer is $((36\ x2)/9)+1 = 9$

D. This question requires you to take the normal formula for calculating communications channels and use it backwards. The formula is $(n(n-1))/2$. So working backwards we can see that the formula will be the answer is $((36\ x2)/9)+1 = 9$

289: The correct answer is C

A. A PowerPoint presentation outlining the major issues will not contain the detailed information the stakeholders are looking for.

B. A summary milestone report will not contain the detailed information that stakeholders are looking for

C. Choosing the most appropriate information and the way in which you deliver it is an important decision to ensure the efficacy of your project reporting.

D. A verbal presentation given casually during a 10 min meeting will not contain the detailed information the stakeholders are looking for.

290: The correct answer is C

A. Decoding is the process that the receiver of message does once the message has been received.

B. Feedback is a process where the receiver provides feedback to the sender of the message to facilitate more effective listening

C. In the standard communications model noise refers to any obstacle in the selected medium between sender and receiver that can impact upon the communication.

D. Transmission is the process of communicating and message via a selected medium.

291: The correct answer is B

A. The questions is asking about the inputs into the Control Communications process and the issue log is an input in this process.
B. The questions is asking about the inputs into the Control Communications process and change requests are an output from, not an input in this process.
C. The questions is asking about the inputs into the Control Communications process and work performance data is an input in this process.
D. The questions is asking about the inputs into the Control Communications process and the project communications are an input in this process.

292: The correct answer is D

A. Budget forecasts are part of earned management which is an example of time series methods, which is the best answer.
B. The judgmental forecasting method uses methods from experts such as the Delphi method.
C. Econometric methods use tools such as linear regression
D. This is an example of a time series method. Earned value is one example of time series method.

293: The correct answer is C

A. Earned value is one example of time series method.
B. Causal is another name for econometric methods which use tools such as linear regression
C. This is an example of using the Delphi technique which is an example of a judgmental forecasting method.
D. Econometric methods use tools such as linear regression

294: The correct answer is A

A. Staff performance review information is not generally included in project performance reports. They would be included team assessments.
B. Current status of risks and issues would definitely be included in a detailed project performance report.

C. The forecasted project completion would definitely be included in a detailed project performance report.

D. A clear summary of changes approved since the last report would definitely be included in a detailed project performance report.

295: The correct answer is C

A. The issue log is an important input into the control communications as it does identify and document what has already happened in the project and provides an effective platform the subsequent communications to be delivered to stakeholders.

B. The issue log is an important input into the control communications as it does identify and document what has already happened in the project and provides an effective platform the subsequent communications to be delivered to stakeholders.

C. The issue log is an important input into the control communications as it does identify and document what has already happened in the project and provides an effective platform the subsequent communications to be delivered to stakeholders.

D. The issue log is an important input into the control communications as it does identify and document what has already happened in the project and provides an effective platform the subsequent communications to be delivered to stakeholders.

296: The correct answer is C

A. It is commonly accepted that communication is key to project success, and that a project manager should always be undertaking communication and that 90% of a project manager's time should be spent on communication with 50% of this time spent communicating

B. It is commonly accepted that communication is key to project success, and that a project manager should always be undertaking communication and that 90% of a project manager's time should be spent on communication with 50% of this time spent communicating with project team.

C. It is commonly accepted that communication is key to project success, and that a project manager should always be undertaking communication and that 90% of a project manager's time should be spent on communication with 50% of this time spent communicating

D. It is commonly accepted that communication is key to project success, and that a project manager should always be undertaking communication and that 90% of a project manager's time should be spent on communication with 50% of this time spent communicating

297: The correct answer is D

A. Is important that the project sponsor and the project manager to have a professional relationship but one of the single biggest reasons project success or failure is appropriate communication.
B. Financial accountability and accuracy will contribute to project failure but a lack of appropriate communication is a larger reason.
C. There are many enterprise environmental factors which can positively and adversely affect the project but appropriate communication is the single biggest reasons for project success or failure.
D. Communication is the essential element if project success. People need to communicate to be effective. It is true that most project problems can be traced back to the lack of appropriate communication.

298: The correct answer is D

A. Risks can be both positive and negative. If they are positive you want them to happen, if they are negative you don't want them to happen.
B. Risks can be both positive and negative. If they are positive you want them to happen, if they are negative you don't want them to happen.
C. Risks can be both positive and negative. If they are positive you want them to happen, if they are negative you don't want them to happen.
D. Risks can be both positive and negative. If they are positive you want them to happen, if they are negative you don't want them to happen.

299: The correct answer is C

A. Is a risk occurs it will have an effect on at least one project objective because if it didn't you wouldn't be interested in it.
B. Risk is an uncertain event or condition and the point of risk management activities is to anticipate this uncertainty to affect its impact on the project.
C. One of the risk strategies available to you is avoidance.
D. Risk is always in the future as once the timeframe for a risk has passed it is no longer worth assessing.

300: The correct answer is D

A. Risk contingency plans deal with unknown risks, not known risks.
B. Risk contingency plans deal with all unknown risks no matter if they are large or small.
C. Risk contingency plans deal with risks that haven't been identified in the risk management plan.
D. Unknown risks which cannot be managed proactively and contingency plans are for unknown risks.

301: The correct answer is B

A. Risk acceptance is a strategy for dealing with risk. It does not refer to the willingness to accept varying degrees of risk
B. The risk tolerance is the degree to which you will or will not accept risk on your project.
C. Risk planning is the process you undertake order to proactively manage uncertainty of a project
D. Risk analysis is one of the tools that you can use to analyze, probability and impact of identified risks.

302: The correct answer is B

A. Due to the fact that risks can occur at any stage in the project you should begin risk management planning as soon as the project is initiated or conceived.
B. Risk can affect a project as soon as it is conceived and you need to be aware, even at a basic level, of the potential impacts of these risks. Risk management occurs throughout the life of the project.
C. Due to the fact that risks can occur at any stage in the project you should begin risk management planning as soon as the project is initiated or conceived.
D. Due to the fact that risks can occur at any stage in the project you should begin risk management planning as soon as the project is initiated or conceived.

303: The correct answer is C

A. This answer is correct as the inputs into the plan risk management process include the project management plan, project charter, stakeholder register, enterprise environmental factors, and organizational process assets.

B. This answer is correct as the inputs into the plan risk management process include the project management plan, project charter, stakeholder register, enterprise environmental factors, and organizational process assets.

C. The risk management plan is the output from the plan risk management process.

D. This answer is correct as the inputs into the plan risk management process include the project management plan, project charter, stakeholder register, enterprise environmental factors, and organizational process assets.

304: The correct answer is B

A. Analytical techniques is one of the three tools and techniques used during the plan risk management process, the other two being expert judgment and meetings.

B. Risk probability and impact assessment is a tool and technique used during the Perform Qualitative Risk Analysis process.

C. Expert judgment is one of the three tools used in the plan risk management process, the other two being analytical techniques and meetings.

D. Meetings are one of the three tools and techniques used in the plan risk management process, the other two being analytical techniques and expert judgment.

305: The correct answer is B

A. The risk assessment register is merely a list of known risks and their assessments . It does not break risks down into categories and subcategories, this is the job of the risk breakdown structure

B. Your risk breakdown structure does what the other breakdown structures do (i.e. WBS and OBS) and takes a high level item and breaks it down into easier to understand and manage subcomponents arranged by category.

C. The probability and impact matrix shows the combined probability and impact of identified risks should they occur on the project. It is the risk breakdown structure it shows the hierarchy of project risks a range by risk category and subcategory

D. The risk register contains information about risk categories, risk events, qualitative risk analysis, quantitative risk analysis, and plan risk responses. It is the risk breakdown structure it shows the hierarchy of project risks a range by risk category

306: The correct answer is A

A. Before qualitatively assessing risks you must have a predetermined and preagreed definition of the different categories to make sure the subjective nature of qualitative analysis is standardized.

B. The purpose of the standardized definitions of risk probability and impact is to assist with the Perform Qualitative Risk Analysis Process, not the Identify Risks process.

C. The purpose of the standardized definitions of risk probability and impact is to assist with the Perform Qualitative Risk Analysis Process, not the Perform Quantitative Risk Analysis process.

D. The purpose of the standardized definitions of risk probability and impact is to assist with the Perform Qualitative Risk Analysis Process, not the Plan Risk Management process.

307: The correct answer is B

A. Perform Qualitative Risk analysis process is performed after the individual risks have been identified in the Identify Risks process.

B. Identify risks is the first stage in the risk management process after you have completed your risk management plan and uses these tools and techniques to prepare the first iteration of the risk register.

C. Perform Quantitative Risk analysis process is performed after the individual risks have been identified in the Identify Risks process.

D. The Plan Risk Management process is the first completed, and produces the risk management plan. It is the Identify Risks process that uses these particular, tools and techniques to produce the first iteration of the risk register.

308: The correct answer is D

A. The Perform Qualitative Risk Analysis process does use a risk register as an input so it knows which risks into the perform qualitative risk analysis upon.

B. The Control Risks process does use the risk register as an input so it knows what risks it is attending the monitor and control

C. The Plan Procurement Management process does use a risk register as an input so it can take into account contract related risks that have been identified.

D. Activity durations estimates are used as an input into the Identify Risks process.

309: The correct answer is B

A. Activity duration estimates are a useful input when identifying risks as they allow you to focus on specific time allowances that may be required.

B. Assumptions analysis is a tool and technique, not an input, used in the Identify Risks process.

C. The stakeholder register is a useful input as it identifies stakeholders, and they can then be asked for input to assist with the identified risks.

D. Activity cost estimates are useful in identifying risks as they provide a quantitative assessment of the risk

310: The correct answer is C

A. Assumptions analysis allows you to document any and all assumptions made as part of the risk of unification process.

B. Risk registers are typically built up using a variety of information gathering techniques, to solicit information from people with experience in your type of project.

C. Risk urgency assessment is a tool and technique from the Perform Qualitative Risk Analysis process.

D. The Delphi technique is a specific type of information gathering techniques

311: The correct answer is C

A. The process flowchart can be used to identify points in a process where risk, or uncertainty is greatest.

B. The cause-and-effect diagram can be used to get to the root cause of any identified risks.

C. A pareto chart is a type of histogram that shows the rank ordering of quality defects by type of category so that corrective action can be focused in the correct place.
D. An influence diagram can show how one risk may impact upon the probability or impact on another risk occurring.

312: The correct answer is A

A. You don't determine probability of risks until completing qualitative and quantitative risk analysis so the first iterations of your list of identified risks may not have probability on them.
B. Your initial list of identified risks will describe individual risk events.
C. Your initial list of identified risks will describe the consequences of individual risk events should they occur.
D. Your initial list of identified risks may describe the known causes of individual risk events.

313: The correct answer is A

A. SWOT stands for strengths, weaknesses, opportunities and threats.
B. Expert judgment Jenny relates to soliciting peoples opinion and experience.
C. PERT analysis is used in other parts of project management, particularly the critical path method and three-point estimating.
D. PEST analysis describes political, economic, social and technological analysis of a particular event or organisation.

314: The correct answer is C

A. The risk register is an essential input into this process as it presents a list of all the identified risks.
B. The risk management plan is an essential input into this process as it outlines how this process will be carried out.
C. The project charter is used as an input into several processes but not the Perform Qualitative Risk Analysis process.
D. The scope baseline is used as an input into this process as it describes the full extent of the work to be completed and not to be completed.

315: The correct answer is D

A. Qualitative risk analysis is done first to prioritize risks quickly and indicate which of these can and should be subject to the more accurate quantitative analysis.
B. Qualitative risk analysis is done first to prioritize risks quickly and indicate which of these can and should be subject to the more accurate quantitative analysis.
C. Qualitative risk analysis is done first to prioritize risks quickly and indicate which of these can and should be subject to the more accurate quantitative analysis.
D. Qualitative risk analysis is done first to prioritize risks quickly and indicate which of these can and should be subject to the more accurate quantitative analysis.

316: The correct answer is A

A. Assessing probability and impact to determine priorities is a characteristic of the qualitative risk analysis process.
B. Quantitative risk analysis uses numerical data of probability and impact to get an assessment of time or dollars.
C. The Identify Risks process is the first of the risk processes that identifies individual risks but does not carry out any assessment of probability or impact.
D. The Plan Risk Management process is the process that outlines how your risk management activities will be executed on the project.

317: The correct answer is A

A. The probability and impact matrix shows the low, medium and high risks on the project.
B. A scatter diagram is generally used during quality management and the plots two variables on the X and Y axis.
C. A Pareto chart lists and hierarchical order the frequency of known events or defects to allow you to assess which 20% of events or defects are causing 80% of the problems.
D. The risk register contains information about risk categories, risk events, qualitative risk analysis, quantitative risk analysis, and plan risk responses. It is the risk breakdown structure it shows the hierarchy of project risks by risk category

318: The correct answer is B

A. Assumptions analysis documents, the assumptions that made during the risk management processes.
B. Since qualitative analysis contains a high degree of subjectivity it is important that you determine the quality of your data you are using.
C. Risk urgency assessment looks at the timeframe for the risk occurring with those risks in the near future deemed to be more urgent than those that may occur further off.
D. Risk categorization is one of the tools that is used to create the risk breakdown structure.

319: The correct answer is C

A. The Plan Risk Responses process develops potential responses to identified risks.
B. Qualitative risk analysis does not use objective numerical data.
C. The key word here is numerical which clearly indicates a quantitative approach.
D. The Identify Risks process is the process where , risk and uncertainty is identified and the risk register is created.

320: The correct answer is B

A. The risk register update is used as an input into the Identify Risks process which in turn has the risk register as an output which is used as an input into the Perform Quantitative Risk Analysis process.
B. The risk register update is used as an input into the Identify Risks process which in turn has the risk register as an output which is used as an input into the Perform Quantitative Risk Analysis process. This is a good example of the iterative nature of projects.
C. The risk register update is used as an input into the Identify Risks process which in turn has the risk register as an output which is used as an input into the Perform Quantitative Risk Analysis process.
D. The risk register update is used as an input into the Identify Risks process which in turn has the risk register as an output which is used as an input into the Perform Quantitative Risk Analysis process.

321: The correct answer is A

A. *Anytime you are using numbers such as dollar values, length of time, or quantifying the impact of risks the three point estimating technique will come in handy.*

B. *Three-point estimating is used in project time management for getting a weighted average of an optimistic, realistic and pessimistic time estimates.*

C. *Three-point estimating are useful tall and risk management quantifying the impacts of risks using an optimistic, realistic and pessimistic assessment of the risk probability or impact.*

D. *Three-point estimating is used in project cost management for getting a weighted average of an optimistic, realistic and pessimistic cost estimates.*

322: The correct answer is A

A. *EMV = total probability x impact = (.4 x $17,000) + (.6 x -$20,000) = $6,800 - $12,000 = -$5,200.*

B. *EMV = total probability x impact = (.4 x $17,000) + (.6 x -$20,000) = $6,800 - $12,000 = -$5,200.*

C. *EMV = total probability x impact = (.4 x $17,000) + (.6 x -$20,000) = $6,800 - $12,000 = -$5,200.*

D. *EMV = total probability x impact = (.4 x $17,000) + (.6 x -$20,000) = $6,800 - $12,000 = -$5,200.*

323: The correct answer is C

A. *EMV = total probability x impact = (.65 x $200,000) + (.35 x -$100,000) = $130,000 - $35,000 = $95,000.*

B. *EMV = total probability x impact = (.65 x $200,000) + (.35 x -$100,000) = $130,000 - $35,000 = $95,000.*

C. *EMV = total probability x impact = (.65 x $200,000) + (.35 x -$100,000) = $130,000 - $35,000 = $95,000.*

D. *EMV = total probability x impact = (.65 x $200,000) + (.35 x -$100,000) = $130,000 - $35,000 = $95,000.*

324: The correct answer is A

A. *This represents the expected monetary value of the risk event occurring.*

B. *This answer is incorrect because it is not a term referenced within the PMBOK® Guide.*

C. *What if analysis is generally performed by a computer and involves complex statistical analysis of events and probabilities.*

D. This may look like the correct answer in the sense that the -$8000 does represent a quantified risk but the correct answer is expected monetary value.

325: The correct answer is D

A. A contingent response strategy is a type of risk response that is triggered by a predefined trigger or event.
B. A management reserve is generally an amount held and controlled by management that projects that encounter completely unforeseeable risk events can apply to use.
C. A slush fund is a common term used by some organizations to describe an amount of money used to various unspecified purposes.
D. A contingency reserve is budget was in the cost baseline is allocated to identified risks that have been assessed quantitatively.

326: The correct answer is A

A. Beta, Normal, and Triangular distributions are all used in quantitative risk analysis. Obtuse distribution is not a term referenced within the PMBOK® Guide.
B. Beta, Normal, and Triangular distributions are all used in quantitative risk analysis.
C. Beta, Normal, and Triangular distributions are all used in quantitative risk analysis.
D. Beta, Normal, and Triangular distributions are all used in quantitative risk analysis.

327: The correct answer is A

A. Sensitivity analysis is the technique to determine the relative impact of a particular risk on independent project variables. A tornado diagram can be used to show the results of the sensitivity analysis.
B. Expected monetary value analysis takes the probability and known numerical impact to determine a financial or time analysis of the risk.
C. A Tornado diagram graphically represents risk areas of the project and the relative degree of uncertainty or sensitivity of each risk category.
D. Modeling and simulation of risk is generally completed by computers as there is statistical analysis that needs to be completed.

328: The correct answer is C

A. Sensitivity analysis is the technique to determine the relative impact of a particular risk on independent project variables. A tornado diagram can be used to show the results of the sensitivity analysis.
B. Expected monetary value analysis takes the probability and known numerical impact to determine a financial or time analysis of the risk.
C. Monte Carlo, or What If, analysis examines a range of possible outcomes from different project variables to present a risk profile for the project.
D. Ishikawa analysis is the process of using a cause-and-effect or fishbone diagram to determine the root cause of risk events

329: The correct answer is A

A. A decision tree analysis sets out in a diagram the various probability of outcomes and value of each outcome so that an overall expected monetary value can be determined.
B. What if scenario analysis uses computer simulations to look at all the potential risk pathways, probability and impact throughout the project to get a likely probability of each risk path.
C. Ishikawa analysis is the process of using a cause-and-effect or fishbone diagram to determine the root cause of risk events
D. A Tornado diagram graphically represents risk areas of the project and the relative degree of uncertainty or sensitivity of each risk category.

330: The correct answer is C

A. Identifying risks is not the next process as it would already been completed in order to get to the stage.
B. Control risks is not the next step as you would first have to plan your risk responses.
C. After identifying your project risks the next step is to plan a response to each one.
D. Execution of the project tasks is not related to whether or not you have completed the process of assessing and documenting risks that may occur on your project.

331: The correct answer is B

A. Risk acceptance is allowing the risk to happen and dealing with it if it occurs.
B. Risk avoidance is eliminating the risk from consideration by doing something that will eliminate it as a possibility.
C. Risk rejection is not a term referenced within the PMBOK® Guide and not one of the appropriate risk response strategies.
D. Risk transfer is transferring the risk to someone other than the project team, such as an insurance company or outside supplier.

332: The correct answer is C

A. This is an example of risk mitigation, risk avoidance would mean building the hydro dam in a less seismically active area.
B. This is an example of risk mitigation, risk. Transfer and would usually be in the form of insurance.
C. Strengthening the dam shows that you are trying to mitigate the damage to the structure should an earthquake occur.
D. This is an example of risk mitigation, acceptance would be taking no action and accepting the consequences should then be struck by an earthquake.

333: The correct answer is D

A. Buying insurance is a process of transferring the impact of the risk to another party.
B. Buying insurance is a process of transferring the impact of the risk to another party.
C. Buying insurance is a process of transferring the impact of the risk to another party.
D. Buying insurance is a process of transferring the impact of the risk to another party.

334: The correct answer is D

A. You can choose to exploit the strengths you have to increase the chances of a positive risk occurring as an acceptable risk response.
B. You can choose to accept positive risks as an acceptable risk response.
C. You can choose to enhance the chances of positive risk occurring as an acceptable risk response.
D. Mitigation is a response to negative risks.

335: The correct answer is A

A. Sharing involves allocating some or all of the ownership of the risk to a third party.
B. Avoidance is a strategy for negative risk response, and the question outlines a positive risk.
C. Mitigation is a strategy for negative risk response, and the question outlines a positive risk.
D. If you were to use and exploit strategy it would, for example, be to appoint senior members of your team to the project.

336: The correct answer is A

A. Planned risk responses represent extra work to be done on the project and as such it must be included in the scope baseline for the project. The scope baseline includes the scope statement, the work breakdown structure and work breakdown structure diction
B. Before beginning any other processes the extra work required and the planned responses should be captured in the scope baseline which includes the work breakdown structure.
C. Before beginning any other processes the extra work required and the planned responses should be captured in the scope baseline which includes the work breakdown structure.
D. Before beginning any other processes the extra work required and the planned responses should be captured in the scope baseline which includes the work breakdown structure.

337: The correct answer is D

A. The specific project documents that will be updated will be. The risk register to include your planned risk responses.
B. Once you have produced your plan risk responses you may need to update several aspects of the project management plan to reflect the plan risk responses.
C. A specific part of the project management plan that may be updated as a result of the plan risk responses will be the cost management plan especially if there are costs associated with your planned risk responses.
D. Contingent response strategies are a technique used in the Plan Risk Response process.

338: The correct answer is B

A. Given that the question outlines that this is a major problem you will not have time to evaluate the risk in any manner and, if you were to do so you would perform qualitative analysis perform quantitative analysis.
B. In this case the risk has occurred and created an impact on the project so there is no need to begin formal evaluation processes. Your risk response plan would identify that a workaround is the best option for unanticipated risks.
C. Given that the question outlines that this is a major problem you will not have time to evaluate the risk in any manner.
D. Given that this has been identified as a major problem your best course of action in this instance is to create a workaround first then contact your project sponsor.

339: The correct answer is A

A. The management reserve is a pool of money controlled by project sponsors and senior management. that is to be used for projects that encounter unforeseeable risks.
B. A contingency reserve is an amount added to a project budget to reflect the quantitative analysis of probability and financial impact of identified risks.
C. A slush fund is a generic term sometimes used by companies to refer to a pool of money used for various purposes not all of which are risk related.
D. The control account is a management control point where scope, budget, actual cost, and schedule are integrated and compute to end value for performance measurement.

340: The correct answer is D

A. This is not an example of exploiting, it is an example of a contingent response strategy being enacted in response to define triggers.
B. This is not an example of risk mitigation, it is an example of a contingent response strategy being enacted in response to defined triggers.
C. This is not an example of transference, it is an example of a contingent response strategy being enacted in response to defined triggers.

D. In this instance your contingent response strategy would have documented that should price increases over what are the estimated that they would constitute a trigger to enact this particular contingent response strategy.

341: The correct answer is B

A. The project management plan is an input into the Control Risks process as it contains several subsidiary plans that will be useful in effectively monitoring and controlling risks.
B. Quality control measurements are not an input into the risk process.
C. In order to effectively control risks you need some sort of information about what is occurring on the project in order to determine if there is a variance between what you planned in relation to risks and what is occurring.
D. The risk register is an essential input into the Control Risks process as it outlines all the identified risks, their probability and impact, and the plan risk responses.

342: The correct answer is A

A. The Control Risks is the process where you continually track the identified risks and look out for new risks.
B. Risk management is the broad term used for the risk management knowledge area.
C. There is no process called risk assessment.
D. There is no process called assess and control risks.

343: The correct answer is A

A. Conducting a risk audit is a useful technique for ensuring that your planned risk responses are effective.
B. Ishikawa, or analysis uses fishbone, or cause-and-effect diagrams to look at root causes of identified effects
C. Risk urgency assessment looks at the timeframe for the risk occurring with those risks in the near future deemed to be more urgent than those that may occur further off.
D. Trend analysis is used to document can determine any trends that may be developing in quality management.

344: The correct answer is A

A. Work performance data is an input into the Control Risks process.
B. As a result of Monitoring and controlling your risks you may detect variance or a need for changes to be made. If so, will raise a change request and submitted by your approved change control process.
C. Particular organizational process assets that will be updated will relate to how the organisation plans and controls risks on projects.
D. Specific parts of the project management plan that will be updated as a result of monitoring and controlling risks will be the risk management plan.

345: The correct answer is D

A. You can be the buyer of goods and services from other providers as part of your procurement strategy on your project.
B. You can be the seller of services responding to some form of request.
C. You can be both buyer and seller of products and services on your project.
D. During procurement management processes you need to be aware that any question on the PMP® exam could indicate your company as either a buyer or a seller of products or services.

346: The correct answer is C

A. The logical order of this knowledge area is to Plan, then Conduct, then Control and finally Close Procurements.
B. The logical order of this knowledge area is to Plan, then Conduct, then Control and finally Close Procurements. Remember though that this knowledge area, like all the others, has a strong iterative component and there will be feedback loops throughout the processes.
C. The logical order of this knowledge area is to Plan, then Conduct, then Control and finally Close Procurements.
D. The logical order of this knowledge area is to Plan, then Conduct, then Control and finally Close Procurements.

347: The correct answer is D

A. Plan Procurement Management is a specific process whereas the Project Procurement management knowledge area includes all the processes referred to in the question.

B. Close Procurements is a specific process whereas the Project Procurement management knowledge area includes all the processes referred to in the question.

C. Project integration management does not specifically address all of these processes.

D. Plan Procurement Management is the knowledge area focused on the processes necessary to purchase or acquire products, services or results from external sources.

348: The correct answer is B

A. A subcontract is a legally binding agreement

B. Organizational process assets do not constitute a legally binding agreement. Depending on the industry, country, context or project type there are many types of legally binding documents in addition to the usual contracts.

C. An agreement when used to mean a legal contract between two or more parties is a legally binding agreement.

D. A purchase order given by a buyer today seller is a legally binding agreement and promised to pay for goods or services rendered.

349: The correct answer is D

A. Your organization's legal team will most likely directly to any organizational process assets that the organisation has.

B. Any lessons learned captured from previous project may give you an insight into what went well and what did not go so well but it will not contain the standards set of rules governing the processes in the organisation.

C. The PMBOK® Guide does not contain a standard set of rules or procuring services from external providers. An organization's process assets would though.

D. The organizational process assets will describe the processes, templates and other documents the organization uses in the procurement process.

350: The correct answer is D

A. *The question clearly states that you have completed the contract work as per the contract specifications. You must enter the Close Procurements process. This process should have provision for any contractual disputes.*
B. *The question clearly states that you have completed the contract work as per the contract specifications. You must enter the Close Procurements process. This process should have provision for any contractual disputes.*
C. *The question clearly states that you have completed the contract work as per the contract specifications. You must enter the Close Procurements process. This process should have provision for any contractual disputes.*
D. *The question clearly states that you have completed the contract work as per the contract specifications. You must enter the Close Procurements process. This process should have provision for any contractual disputes.*

351: The correct answer is A

A. *The term entrepreneur is never used to describe the buyer in a contract. The term buyer is a very formal way of describing a variety of more usual descriptions. This is one of those situations where you may need to translate a formal the PMBOK® Guide term*
B. *Your client is one good example of a buyer in a contract, and your organisation would be the seller.*
C. *Somebody requesting services from you is a good example of a buyer in a contract.*
D. *The prime contractor to a contract will go on to buy services and goods from other sellers, and as such they are buyer in a contract.*

352: The correct answer is B

A. *The vendor is simply another way of saying seller.*
B. *The term seller is a very formal way of describing a variety of more usual descriptions. This is one of those situations where you may need to translate a formal the PMBOK® Guide term into one you use more regularly.*
C. *A service provider will sell goods or services to a buyer*
D. *A contractor will provide goods and services to the buyer in contract and as such they are a seller.*

353: The correct answer is B

A. *The activity resource requirements is the useful place for you to be able to determine whether there are particular resources you will have to procure from external providers*

B. *Make-or-buy decisions are an output of the Plan Procurement Management process. It is worth noting that with 11 inputs this process is the one with the most inputs.*

C. *The stakeholder register will provide useful information on individual stakeholders and their interest in the project, particularly as they relate to contractual decisions.*

D. *Your requirements documentation will be a very valuable input into this process as it will outline any contractual or legal implications that need to be taken into consideration when making procurement decisions.*

354: The correct answer is D

A. *Cost plus incentive fee forms of contract are a popular form of contract but the most popular form of contract is the firm fixed-price contract.*

B. *Time and materials form of contract are generally only used the small or emergency works and as such are not the most common form of procurement contract.*

C. *Fixed price incentive fee forms of contract are a popular form of contract but the most popular form of contract is the firm fixed-price contract.*

D. *The firm fixed price is the most common form of procurement contract.*

355: The correct answer is C

A. *In a fixed-price contract the supplier is obligated to deliver the contracted-for item at a fixed price. The supplier is aware of the risk and will put an allowance for the risk in the contracted price.*

B. *In a fixed-price contract the supplier is obligated to deliver the contracted-for item at a fixed price. The supplier is aware of the risk and will put an allowance for the risk in the contracted price. This often means that the project team will pay the supplier for the cost of the risk regardless of whether the risk occurs.*

C. *In a fixed-price contract the supplier is obligated to deliver the contracted-for item at a fixed price. The supplier is aware of the risk and will put an allowance for the risk in the contracted price. D. In a fixed-price contract the supplier is obligated to deliver the contracted-for item at a fixed price. The supplier is aware of the risk and will put an allowance for the risk in the contracted price.*

356: *The correct answer is B*

A. *All this may seem to be the technically correct thing to do it will cause major problems for your project and also the contractor. You would be better off making provision to pay the contractor by negotiating a change to the contract.*
B. *Although it is not to exactly to the letter of the contract, you are going to have much more trouble if the seller cannot make the payroll and cannot complete the contract because their employees will not work without pay. The best thing would be to change the contract in some way that is mutually beneficial. This is not really a procurement question but an ethical one although there is considerable overlap.*
C. *You may end up paying for work, is today but you must first negotiate a change to the current contract to allow such payments to the contractor.*
D. *You may end up paying for work, is today but you must first negotiate a change to the current contract to allow such payments to the contractor.*

357: *The correct answer is B*

A. *Of all the options presented the cost plus incentive fee is the one that puts least risk on the seller. Any form of fixed price contract places or risk on the seller and the buyer.*
B. *The type of contract selected will reflect which party adopts the most risk for carrying out the work. The seller prefers one where the price is not fixed. In fact would probably prefer to work with a time and materials contract but it is not one of the options presented.*
C. *Of all the options presented the cost plus incentive fee is the one that puts least risk on the seller. Any form of fixed price contract places or risk on the seller and the buyer.*
D. *Of all the options presented the cost plus incentive fee is the one that puts least risk on the seller. Any form of fixed price contract places or risk on the seller and the buyer.*

358: *The correct answer is C*

A. *Fixed-price with incentive fee is best when the scope of work can be fully defined.*
B. *Time and materials is best for small work or emergency works.*

C. Where the scope or work is not fully defined a cost reimbursable contract such as cost plus fixed fee is the best for both seller and buyer as it allows for continued development of the scope.

D. Any form of fixed price contract is best in the scope of work can be fully defined.

359: The correct answer is A

A. A time and materials contract is suitable where the work is urgent or where the scope of work is largely undefined.

B. Given that the situation question is urgent and requires immediate attention you do not have the time to go through the process of negotiating any form of fixed price contract therefore a time and materials contract is best.

C. Given that the situation question is urgent and requires immediate attention you do not have the time to go through the process of negotiating any form of cost reimbursable contract therefore a time and materials contract is best.

D. Given that the situation question is urgent and requires immediate attention you do not have the time to go through the process of negotiating any form of cost reimbursable contract therefore a time and materials contract is best.

360: The correct answer is B

A. A request for proposal is a form of procurement, document, that goes to potential sellers outlining the work required and asking for a response from them.

B. Request for fixed price contract is not a term referenced within the PMBOK® Guide.

C. A request for quotation is a form of procurement, document that goes to potential sellers asking for a quote for a prescribed scope of work

D. A request for information is a former procurement, document it goes to all potential sellers requesting information about the seller, their capabilities, and the organisation.

361: The correct answer is D

A. The source selection criteria, which outline how you will select potential sellers is an output from the Plan Procurement Management process.

B. The procurement statement of work, which describes the work to be completed as part of the contract is an output of the Plan Procurement Management process.

C. The procurement management plan is the primary output from the Plan Procurement Management process.

D. The project scope statement is not an output from the Plan Procurement Management process. It is an output from the Define Scope process

362: The correct answer is D

A. Expert judgment as a tool or technique used to solicit information with people with experience in a particular area.

B. Risk related contract decisions would be completed as part of project risk management and not as part of make-or-buy analysis

C. Source selection criteria are other criteria you developed to help you choose which sellers will be invited to be part of the procurement process and how successful sellers will be selected.

D. Make-or-buy analysis is exactly what it says it is. The decision to make something in house or buy it from outside the organization.

363: The correct answer is A

A. Make-or-buy decisions are an output of the Plan Procurement Management process.

B. Technical capability would most certainly be one of the criteria by which you would judge potential sellers.

C. Management approach would most certainly be one of the criteria by which you would judge potential sellers.

D. The issue of proprietary rights and who owns the service or goods produced as a result of the contract would most certainly be one of the criteria by which you would judge potential sellers.

364: The correct answer is C

A. The Close Procurements process is focused on making sure that all contract used in the project are successfully closed.

B. *The Plan Procurement Management process produces the procurement management plan and the procurement statement of work which are then used to assist the Control Procurement process, which is the correct answer.*

C. *The Conduct Procurement process is where you put into practice the process of acquiring external contractors outlined in your procurement management plan.*

D. *The Control Procurements process is focused upon checking whether the procurement management plan is working and, if any changes are required.*

365: The correct answer is D

A. *The project management plan, particularly the procurement management plan will be an essential input to help you carry out the planned work in procurements.*

B. *Source selection criteria are other criteria you developed to help you choose which sellers will be invited to be part of the procurement process and how successful sellers will be selected.*

C. *The procurement statement of work is an essential input as it describes the work to be done as part of contract.*

D. *Resource calendars are an output from the Conduct Procurements process.*

366: The correct answer is B

A. *A bidder conference is a real and virtual meeting of all sellers bidding to be part of the contract.*

B. *It is not uncommon for organizations to have a predetermined list of sellers who are qualified to offer services or products in a particular area. Inclusion on the list is usually dependent on prior experience or meeting defined criteria.*

C. *The procurement management plan is an output from the Plan Procurement Management process and it outlines how you will carry out your project procurement.*

D. *Proposal evaluation techniques assist you to evaluate responses from sellers.*

367: The correct answer is D

A. Procurement negotiations are carried out prior to signing the contract.
B. A weighted average calculation would be used in something like three point estimating.
C. Expert judgment is a tool or technique that is used to solicit information from people with experience in a particular area.
D. It is common to have a predetermined set of criteria to assess response from sellers. The buying organization may decide to give greater or less weight to certain of these criteria depending on the circumstances.

368: The correct answer is A

A. A bidding conference should be fair to all those involved in the process. In this instance the seller is not doing anything unethical and it is up to you to ensure that all sellers hear the question and answer.
B. You should refuse to provide an answer to the seller right then but you should make it clear that you will provide an answer to all sellers.
C. You should not provide an answer that just that seller, instead, you should provide an answer to all sellers.
D. What the seller has done is not an ethical as long as it is handled correctly they do not need to be removed from the room or process.

369: The correct answer is B

A. Conduct Procurements is the process of procuring goods and services from external sellers.
B. The Control Procurements process if completed as part of the Monitoring and Controlling process group. Both parties in a contract will administer the contract to ensure the other party of completing the work as per the contract documentation.
C. Close Procurements is the process of making sure that all contracts used on the project are closed.
D. Plan Procurement Management Is the process that produces the procurement management plan and the procurement statement of work.

370: The correct answer is D

A. The Direct and Manage Project Work provides work performance data is an input into the control procurements process.
B. The Monitor and Control Project Work provides work performance reports as an input into the control procurements process.

C. The Perform Integrated Change Control provides approved change requests as an input into the control procurements process.

D. The Control Procurements process requires a lot of information from other processes to ensure you are capable to judging whether or not the other party to a contract is fulfilling their obligations. Control Costs is not one of these processes.

371: The correct answer is C

A. Inspections and audits are a tool and technique used to ensure that both the processes outlined in the contract and the expected deliverable of the contract are being delivered as per the terms of contract.

B. Performance reporting is a valuable tool to use during the Control Procurements process as it allows you to determine whether the terms of the contract are being met as planned.

C. Work performance information is an input, not a tool or technique, into the Control Procurements process.

D. Claims administration is a tool and technique for dealing with any disputes over the terms of contracts.

372: The correct answer is D

A. You must first complete the Close Procurements process before completing the Close Project process as contract closure comes before project closure.

B. The Close Project process and Close Procurements process are separate and distinct processes. You must first complete the Close Procurements process before completing the Close Project process

C. You must first complete the Close Procurements process before completing the Close Project process as contract closure comes before project closure.

D. A contract is just one part of a project and as such before you can close the project you need to ensure that all the contracts are closed.

373: The correct answer is D

A. This is a tricky question that you may have had difficulty answering. The question itself does not give a lot of information about why the general manager has decided to terminate the contract so we must assume it is for legitimate reasons in which case t

B. You may do this as part of closing your procurement but the best answer is to begin the Close Procurements process.

C. This may end up being part of your lessons learned process are the best answer is to begin the Close Procurements process.

D. This is a tricky question that you may have had difficulty answering. The question itself does not give a lot of information about why the general manager has decided to terminate the contract so we must assume it is for legitimate reasons in which case t

374: The correct answer is C

A. A procurement audit is a structured review of the procurement management process from the beginning to the end to see whether it was followed, whether it was appropriate, and whether there are any improvements could be made.

B. Not all contracts end cleanly and any instances where Procurement negotiations and negotiated settlements are an effective tool or technique to use during this process.

C. Bidder conferences are a tool from the Conduct Procurements process.

D. Records Management system as a tool and technique used in the Close Procurements process to manage contract. Procurement documentation and records with archiving.

375: The correct answer is D

A. Given that contracts are a formal written form of communication that is best that all communication about the contract as in the same formal written form.

B. Given that contracts are a formal written form of communication that is best that all communication about the contract as in the same formal written form.

C. Given that contracts are a formal written form of communication that is best that all communication about the contract as in the same formal written form.

D. A contract is a formal written document and all correspondence about the contract should also be completed in a formal written format.

376: The correct answer is C

A. To calculate the point of total assumption you need to use the following formula: ((Ceiling Price - Target Price)/Buyers share ration) + Target Cost) which gives a point of total assumption of $125,000.
B. To calculate the point of total assumption you need to use the following formula: ((Ceiling Price - Target Price)/Buyers share ration) + Target Cost) which gives a point of total assumption of $125,000.
C. To calculate the point of total assumption you need to use the following formula: ((Ceiling Price - Target Price)/Buyers share ration) + Target Cost) which gives a point of total assumption of $125,000.
D. To calculate the point of total assumption you need to use the following formula: ((Ceiling Price - Target Price)/Buyers share ration) + Target Cost) which gives a point of total assumption of $125,000.

377: The correct answer is A

A. It is doubtful that you would be able to document the personal conflict resolution style of stakeholders. Having a thorough stakeholder analysis completed early in the project is an effective aid into several processes. When analyzing stakeholders you sho
B. As part of identifying stakeholders. You should also identify and document their expectations of the project so that you can effectively manage them.
C. As part of identifying stakeholders you should identify and document the influence on the project.
D. As part of identifying stakeholders. You should identify and document their interest in the project.

378: The correct answer is C

A. Procurement documents are used as an input into the identify stakeholders process because parties to the contract are key project stakeholders.
B. The project charter is used as an input into the identify stakeholders process because it can provide information about internal and external parties relate with the project
C. The stakeholder register is an output from the Identify Stakeholders process.
D. Lessons learned, which are part of organizational process assets, are an important input into the identify stakeholders process.

379: The correct answer is B

A. The stakeholder management strategy is not term found in the PMBOK® Guide, although it may be a commonly used term it does not analyze stakeholder impact and interest in the project

B. You are completing stakeholder analysis. You may choose to show the results in a diagram such as a Power/Interest grid which shows the relative power and interest in the project each stakeholder has.

C. This answer is incorrect because stakeholder register assimilation is not a term referenced within the PMBOK® Guide

D. Although this answer may sound correct the best answer is stakeholder analysis

380: The correct answer is C

A. A stakeholder register templates is an organizational process asset for listing and documenting information about stakeholders.

B. A control chart is a tool used in the project quality management

C. A Power/interest grid plots the relative power and interest each identified stakeholder has in your project.

D. The salience model maps the degree of power, urgency, and legitimacy that each stakeholder has.

381: The correct answer is D

A. A simple e-mail distribution list may be part of your communications plan but it would certainly not document all stakeholders on the project.

B. Your organizational process assets may include a blank stakeholder register that if you wish to get the information you are seeking in this question the stakeholder register is the best answer

C. The stakeholder management strategy, if such a thing exists, would not document who the individual stakeholders are.

D. The stakeholder register contains all the information you know about all stakeholders on the project.

382: The correct answer is C

A. The stakeholder register documents each stakeholder and their interest in the project. It is not the best answer to this question as the stakeholder analysis matrix analyses the impact and interest each stakeholder has upon project.

B. This answer is incorrect because the term is too vague, the correct term is stakeholder analysis matrix.

C. A stakeholder analysis matrix lists the stakeholders, their potential impact and assessment and also potential strategies for dealing with any impact on the project.

D. This answer is incorrect because it is not a term referenced within the PMBOK® Guide.

383: The correct answer is B

A. The communications management plan is not used as an input into the Plan Quality Management process

B. Communication with stakeholders represents a positive risk if done effectively and a negative risk if done poorly and as such, the communications management plan is an important input into the Manage Stakeholder Engagement process

C. The communications management plan is not used as an input into the Estimate Costs process

D. The communications management plan is not used as an input into the Close Project or Phase process

384: The correct answer is A

A. Managing stakeholder engagement is one of the most important processes a project manager can focus upon to contribute to project success.

B. The Manage Communications process is focused on creating collecting and distributing and storing of project information in accordance with the communications management plan.

C. Stakeholder analysis is a tool and technique not a process.

D. Control communications is focused on monitoring and controlling communications throughout the project.

385: The correct answer is D

A. This would not solve the issue as The problem is that you are paying too much attention to the cost and time metrics and not paying enough attention to what it is that stakeholders consider to be a measure of success.
B. Quitting the project would not be what a professional project manager would do. The problem is that you are paying too much attention to the cost and time metrics and not paying enough attention to what it is that stakeholders consider to be a measure of success. By revisiting your communications management plan, especially the manage stakeholder process you will increase the probability of project success.
C. Saying nothing would be withdrawing from the problem and not on a professional project manager would do. The problem is that you are paying too much attention to the cost and time metrics and not paying enough attention to what it is that stakeholders con
D. The problem is that you are paying too much attention to the cost and time metrics and not paying enough attention to what it is that stakeholders consider to be a measure of success.

386: The correct answer is B

A. With any of the activities undertaken in association with managing, and identifying stakeholder expectations. Your primary goal is to get stakeholders to support your project. Failing this your goal should be to ensure they do not oppose the project.
B. With any of the activities undertaken in association with managing, and identifying stakeholder expectations. Your primary goal is to get stakeholders to support your project. Failing this your goal should be to ensure they do not oppose the project.
C. With any of the activities undertaken in association with managing, and identifying stakeholder expectations. Your primary goal is to get stakeholders to support your project. Failing this your goal should be to ensure they do not oppose the project.
D. With any of the activities undertaken in association with managing, and identifying stakeholder expectations. Your primary goal is to get stakeholders to support your project. Failing this your goal should be to ensure they do not oppose the project.

387: The correct answer is A

A. The purpose of stakeholder analysis is to document information about individual stakeholders, their interest in the project, and their impact on the project so that you are able to influence them if required.
B. Expert judgment as a tool and technique used to solicit information from people with experience in a particular area.
C. There are several information gathering techniques, all of which are used to gather information from subject matter experts, technicians, subject matter experts and other stakeholders with information you require on the project.
D. Meetings are an effective communications and information distribution tool but they are not related assessing attributes about individual stakeholders.

388: The correct answer is B

A. The power/interest grid is used to classify stakeholders based on the amount of power and interest they have on the project
B. The salience model is used to describe classes of stakeholders based on their power, urgency, and legitimacy.
C. The influence/impact grid is used to classify stakeholders based on the amount of influence and impact they have on the project.
D. A Pareto chart is used primarily during quality management to determine which 20% of the issues cause 80% of problems.

389: The correct answer is A

A. Classifying stakeholders by the level of engagement according to them being either unaware, resistant, neutral, support of leading is an example of an analytical techniques used during the Plan Stakeholder Management process.
B. This is not an example of information gathering techniques. There are several information gathering techniques, all of which are used to gather information from subject matter experts, technicians, subject matter experts and other stakeholders with information you require on the project.
C. The question outlines a situation in which you are using a specific form of analytical technique to carry out stakeholder analysis. The best answer is analytical techniques.
D. Expert judgment as a tool and technique used to solicit information from people with experience in a particular area.

390: The correct answer is A

A. This answer is correct because management skills include the ability to facilitate consensus toward project objectives, influence stakeholders to support the project, negotiate agreements to satisfy the project needs, and modify organizational behavior
B. The best answer to this question is management skills which are a specific subset of interpersonal skills that facilitate consensus toward project objectives, influence stakeholders to support the project, negotiate agreements to satisfy the project needs, and modify or organizational behavior to accept project outcomes.
C. This is not an example of communications methods. It is an example of management skills.
D. This is not an example of information gathering techniques. There are several information gathering techniques, all of which are used to gather information from subject matter experts, technicians, subject matter experts and other stakeholders with information

391: The correct answer is B

A. Manage Stakeholder Engagement is the process of Working with the stakeholder management plan and communicating in working with stakeholders to ensure their needs and objectives.
B. Control Stakeholder Engagement is the process focused on monitoring overall project stakeholder relationships, engagement, satisfaction and adjusting your stakeholder engagement strategies to ensure they remain effective.
C. Control Communications is the process of checking, monitoring and controlling your project communications against the communication management plan.
D. Manage Communications is the process of preparing to create, collect, and distribute project information in accordance with the communications management plan.

392: The correct answer is C

A. This question is asking about the types of organizational process assets updates that may be done as a result of the Control Stakeholder Engagement process are being carried out.

B. This question is asking about the types of organizational process assets updates that may be done as a result of the Control Stakeholder Engagement process are being carried out. The specific organizational process assets that may be updated as a result of carrying this process out our stakeholder notifications, project reports, project presentations, project records, feedback from stakeholders, and lessons learned documentation.
C. The issue log is not an organizational process asset, it is a project document .This question is asking about the types of organizational process assets updates that may be done as a result of the Control Stakeholder Engagement process
D. This question is asking about the types of organizational process assets updates that may be done as a result of the Control Stakeholder Engagement process are being carried out.

393: The correct answer is B

A. Complying with the professional code of ethics means reporting ethical, professional or legal violations to the appropriate authority. In this case the appropriate authority is the Project Management Institute.
B. Complying with the professional code of ethics means reporting Ethical, professional or legal violations to the appropriate authority. In this case the appropriate authority is the Project Management Institute.
C. Complying with the professional code of ethics means reporting ethical, professional or legal violations to the appropriate authority. In this case the appropriate authority is the Project Management Institute.
D. Complying with the professional code of ethics means reporting ethical, professional or legal violations to the appropriate authority. In this case the appropriate authority is the Project Management Institute.

394: The correct answer is B

A. Your best course of action is always to be up front and honest with information as soon as you become aware of it. In this instance you should first inform the project sponsor.
B. Your best course of action is always to be up front and honest with information as soon as you become aware of it. In this instance you should first inform the project sponsor.
C. Your best course of action is always to be up front and honest with information as soon as you become aware of it. In this instance you should first inform the project sponsor.

D. Your best course of action is always to be up front and honest with information as soon as you become aware of it. In this instance you should first inform the project sponsor.

395: The correct answer is D

A. You should not assign him lower level tasks and bring in another more qualified person because you have an professional obligation to ensure people have the right amount of training to complete their job.
B. You cannot simply do nothing and assume that he will learn on the job. You have an professional obligation to ensure people have the right amount of training to complete their job.
C. You cannot simply assign the project administrator to another project. You have an professional obligation to ensure people have the right amount of training to complete their job.
D. You have an professional obligation to ensure people have the right amount of training to complete their job.

396: The correct answer is A

A. In this instance you must not give wrong information to the stakeholders so you must reschedule the meeting to give you time to fix the errors.
B. It is important that you always present accurate information so you should reschedule the meeting to give you time to fix the errors.
C. Although this answer seems like a noble thing to do your first commitment to providing accurate information see cannot table the report to the meeting. You should reschedule the meeting to give you time to fix the error is.
D. As project manager you are ultimately responsible for information presented to project stakeholders. Your best course of action is to reschedule the meeting give you time to fix the errors.

397: The correct answer is D

A. To accept Any form of payment would be unethical. Your only choice is to refuse the payment and let you project sponsor or manager know that it was offered.

B. To accept payment would be unethical even if you then did divided amongst the team members. Your only choice is to refuse the payment and let you project sponsor or manager know that it was offered.
C. To accept payment would be unethical. Your only choice is to refuse the payment and let you project sponsor or manager know that it was offered.
D. To accept payment would be unethical. Your only choice is to refuse the payment and let you project sponsor or manager know that it was offered.

398: The correct answer is B

A. You cannot submit a report based on what you believe next month figures will be. In order to be a professional and ethical project manager you are required to show honesty at all levels of the profession and in all instances.
B. In order to be a professional and ethical project manager you are required to show honesty at all levels of the profession and in all instances.
C. Resigning from the project is an extreme action to take. You should first explained your project sponsor the reasons why you believe the project reporting should always be honest. In order to be a professional and ethical project manager you are required
D. Your first step should be to explain to your project sponsor the reasons why you believe the project reporting should be honest.

399: The correct answer is B

A. Given that there are some disparity between team members and their contribution to the project the best way to address this issue would be asked to team members how they would divide the money.
B. Probably the best thing to do in this situation would be to divide the money by letting the team decide how to divide it. This is an example of participative management and good leadership. It acknowledges that your efforts and successes were a result not just of your efforts that of your teams.
C. Probably the best thing to do in this situation would be to divide the money by letting the team decide how to divide it. This is an example of participative management and good leadership. It acknowledges that your efforts and successes were a result not
D. Given that there are some disparity between team members and their contribution to the project the best way to address this issue would be asked to team members how they would divide the money.

400: The correct answer is C

A. It would be difficult to get a change request approved for a deliberate error in the project. Instead, you should record the discrepancy, inform the customer and look for ways to ensure the project won't be affected.
B. Given that you have formed the opinion that the era will probably not affect the functionality the final software product. It would not make sense to stop the project and start again. You would need to record the discrepancy and inform the customer of the issue.
C. In this instance the best solution is to record the issue and make an effort to remedy it to the satisfaction of all parties.
D. You cannot simply ignore the problem. In this instance the best solution is to record the issue and make an effort to remedy it to the satisfaction of all parties.

401: The correct answer is C

A. You should not present your own presentation as the invitation has been extended to your project sponsor. This course of action is to explain to your sponsor of intellectual property belongs to the author of the property. If you create a presentation base
B. Intellectual property belongs to the author of the property. If you create a presentation based on your own work, you have a right to receive credit for it.
C. Intellectual property belongs to the author of the property. If you create a presentation based on your own work, you have a right to receive credit for it.
D. For meeting with the project sponsors manager you should explain to the sponsor that the correct thing to do is to acknowledge all authors and contribute to the work.

402: The correct answer is D

A. Reporting the official to his manager will probably do no good as bribery is probably ingrained within the culture.
B. It doesn't matter how the money is paid at no time can you pay a bribe. A bribe is an illegal payment regardless of accepted custom.
C. At no time can you pay a bribe. A bribe is an illegal payment regardless of accepted custom.

D. At no time can you pay a bribe. A bribe is an illegal payment regardless of accepted custom.

403: The correct answer is A

A. The questions does not say that the fee is a bribe. As such you can go ahead and pay it if your project has allowed for it. If not you may wish to submit a change request to acquire the funds needed.
B. The question does not say that this is the bribe. It clearly says that it is a processing fee so you should assume that it is a legal form of fee to rush applications
C. You should not walk out of the meeting and notify your project sponsor because the question does not say that this is the bribe. It clearly says that it is a processing fee so you should assume that it is a legal form of fee to rush applications
D. There is no need to hide the transaction because it is a legal fee that he is requesting in order to rush your application.

404: The correct answer is A

A. You should inform the other party at the meeting have been postponed for at least three days. You must act ethically at all times and clearly there is no way you can act in good faith if the meeting goes ahead.
B. You should inform the other party at the meeting have been postponed for at least three days. You must act ethically at all times and clearly there is no way you can act in good faith if the meeting goes ahead.
C. You should inform the other party at the meeting have been postponed for at least three days. You must act ethically at all times and clearly there is no way you can act in good faith if the meeting goes ahead.
D. Cancelling the meeting and telling the other party why may cause a rift in the relationship if the project does go ahead. You should inform the other party at the meeting have been postponed for at least three days. You must act ethically at all times and

ABOUT THE AUTHOR

Sean Whitaker, BA, MSc, MBA, PMP has a diverse project management background having successfully managed complex projects in the construction, telecommunications and IT industries. He brings this diversity of experience into sharp focus with his emphasis on professional and appropriate, or practically perfect, project management.

Sean regularly teaches and speaks about professional project management, and has been a long term volunteer with the Project Management Institute. He is also the co-founder of Falcon Training, one of the world's best project management training companies. Sean is also the author of "PMP® Training Kit", "PMP® Rapid Review", & "The Practically Perfect Project Manager" available from all good book retailers. He has also developed the 3PM project management methodology.

When not pursuing his professional passion of project management Sean is an accomplished musician.

www.seanwhitaker.com

www.falcontraining.com

6944330R00158

Printed in Great Britain
by Amazon.co.uk, Ltd.,
Marston Gate.